TO BE MODERN

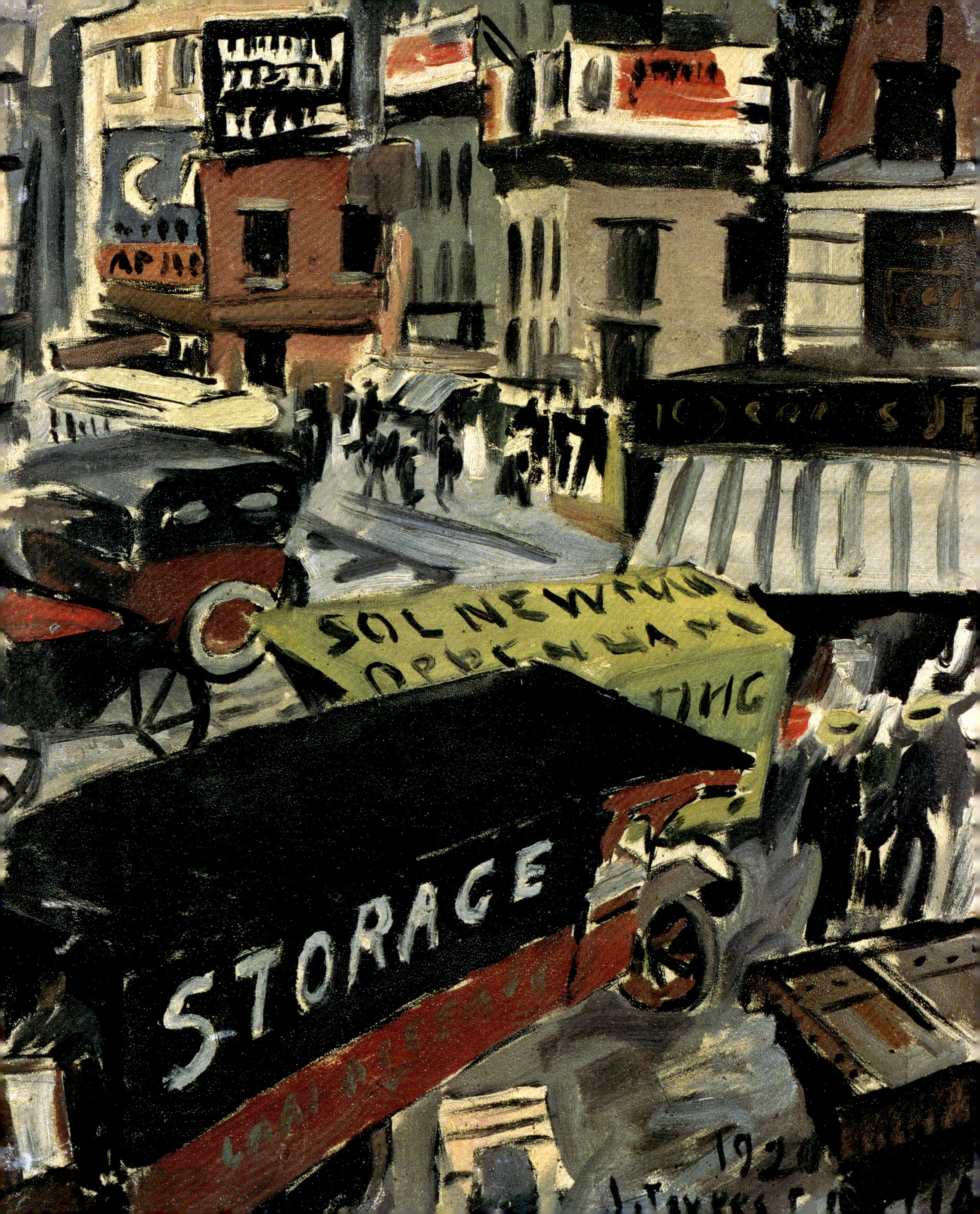
STORAGE
1920

Sylvia Yount
Elizabeth Johns

TO BE MODERN

AMERICAN ENCOUNTERS WITH CEZANNE AND COMPANY

Museum of American Art of the Pennsylvania Academy of the Fine Arts
Distributed by University of Pennsylvania Press

Frontispiece: Joaquín Torres-Garcia, *Fourteenth Street,* 1920, oil on board, 22 x 18", Courtesy of CDS Gallery, New York.

Front cover, detail: Stanton Macdonald-Wright, *Aeroplane Synchromy in Yellow-Orange*, 1920, oil on canvas, 24 ¼ x 24", The Metropolitan Museum of Art, Alfred Stieglitz Collection, 1949. Copyright ©1995 by The Metropolitan Museum of Art.

Back cover: Marguerite Zorach, *The Connoisseur,* 1910–11, oil on canvas, 22 x 17 ½", Collection of Mr. and Mrs. Meyer P. Potamkin.

Published on the occasion of the exhibition "To Be Modern: American Encounters with Cézanne and Company," organized by the Museum of American Art of the Pennsylvania Academy of the Fine Arts.

The exhibition and this accompanying book were made possible in part by the generosity of Mr. and Mrs. Meyer P. Potamkin and Advanta.

Museum of American Art of the Pennsylvania Academy
of the Fine Arts
Philadelphia, Pa.
June 15–September 29, 1996

Curator: Sylvia Yount
Editor: Gerald Zeigerman
Design: Meghan Alonzo and Phillip Unetic
Printing: Meridian Printing

118 North Broad Street
Philadelphia, Pa. 19102

Distributed by University of Pennsylvania Press.

Printed in the United States.

Library of Congress Cataloguing-in-Publication Data

Yount, Sylvia
To Be Modern: American Encounters with Cézanne and Company / Sylvia Yount. Elizabeth Johns.
p. cm.
Exhibition organized by the Museum of American Art of the Pennsylvania Academy of the Fine Arts.
ISBN 0-943836-18-2
1. Modernism (Art)—United States—Exhibitions. 2. Art, American—Exhibitions. 3. Art, Modern—20th century—United States—Exhibitions. 4. Pennsylvania Academy of the Fine Arts—Influence. 5. Cézanne, Paul, 1839–1906. I. Johns, Elizabeth, 1963– .
II. Pennsylvania Academy of the Fine Arts. Museum of American Art. III. Title.
N6512.5.M63Y68 1996
709' .73'07474811—dc20 96-15561
CIP

Contents

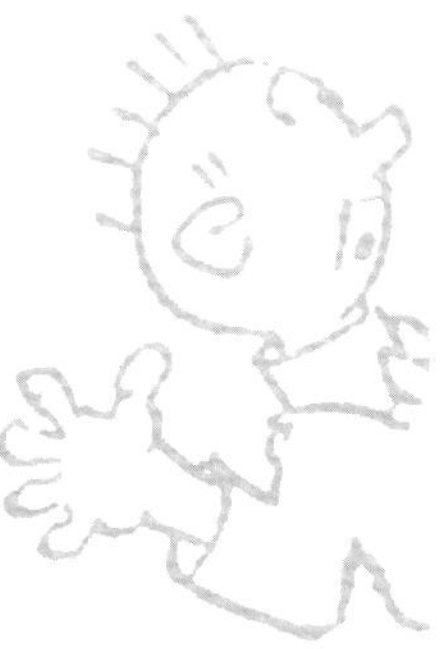

Acknowledgments

I wish to thank the lenders, public and private, whose willingness to share their works has made this exhibition possible. I am particularly indebted to Mr. and Mrs. Meyer P. Potamkin and the staff of the Philadelphia Museum of Art—especially Marge Klein, of Twentieth-Century Art, and Laura Steward, of Prints, Drawings, and Photographs—for their generous contributions and assistance.

For early encouragement of the exhibition concept, I wish to recognize Linda Bantel; Gresham Riley, president, Pennsylvania Academy of the Fine Arts; and Jo Joslyn, assistant director, University of Pennsylvania Press. Moreover, I am very grateful to Elizabeth Johns, friend and mentor, for her counsel and collaboration on this publication. Gerald Zeigerman's meticulous editing and good humor deserve high praise, as does the innovative design work of Phillip Unetic and Meghan Alonzo.

Elizabeth Kennedy provided crucial research assistance in both exhibition and publication planning. Cheryl Leibold guided me through the Academy's rich archives and offered valuable comments on the catalogue manuscript. The Academy's librarian, Marietta Boyer, was unfailingly generous in her research support. Thanks are due as well to Abraham Davidson and Ben Wolf for sharing their knowledge of Philadelphia's "moderns."

Also at the Academy, Gale Rawson, museum registrar; Mark Bockrath, chief conservator; Barbara Katus, manager of rights and reproductions; and Anna Welch and Marion McParland, public relations, merit special attention for their talents and professionalism, as do all of my museum colleagues. Indeed, my greatest debt is to the unique historical legacy and resources of the Academy itself, an extraordinary trove of objects and ideas.

Sylvia Yount

I acknowledge with gratitude the practical help of Kena Frank, my research assistant; the ongoing pleasure of exchange with Sylvia Yount; and the intellectual stimulation of students in my graduate seminars on early American modernism at the University of Pennsylvania: Rachael Arauz, Katie Bourguignon, Judith Dolkart, Kristin Fedders, Asya Haikin, Elizabeth Kennedy, Huon Su Kwon, Janine Mileaf, Nancy Miller, Eric Perry, Shelley Pyne-Henley, Jon Seydl, and Anna Sloan.

Elizabeth Johns

Foreword

Empathy may provide the most insightful window into the character and substance of history, and it may also be the best way to understand, in our postmodern age, what it meant "to be modern" in the unsettled years that followed the First World War. Many of the cultural innovations we take for granted today were a novelty to the majority of Americans in 1921, the year in which the Pennsylvania Academy of the Fine Arts hosted the remarkable exhibition with the unremarkable title, "Exhibition of Paintings and Drawings Showing the Later Tendencies in Art."

The Museum of American Art's "To Be Modern: American Encounters with Cézanne and Company" is a partial reconstruction of this 1921 exhibition. It brings together ninety-eight works by forty-eight artists, roughly one-quarter of which were included in the "Later Tendencies" effort, an exhibition that featured 280 objects. Because the alternative title for this 1921 show specified the inclusion of uniquely *American* artists, it provided a very different focus from the 1913 Armory Show, in which the Europeans sensationally overwhelmed the Americans. To the generation of 1921, modernity suggested a more dynamic relationship to the culture of Europe and acknowledged a creative tension among the lapsing avant-garde, embodied by Arthur B. Davies, William Glackens, and John Sloan; the European-inspired avant-garde, represented by John Covert, Stanton Macdonald-Wright, Man Ray, and Max Weber; and a distinctly American avant-garde, nascent in the work of such disparate artists as Thomas Hart Benton, Arthur G. Dove, John Marin, and Georgia O'Keeffe.

"To Be Modern" was conceived by Dr. Sylvia Yount, Curator of Collections at the Museum of American Art. She is to be commended for organizing this ambitious exhibition and catalogue and for understanding with such acuity the importance of its prototype as a watershed event in the history of American modernism. The project has been significantly enriched by the scholarship and eloquence of Dr. Elizabeth Johns, Silfen Term Professor of the History of Art at the University of Pennsylvania; her contribution to this catalogue conveys the intellectual excitement of the period. In addition, we wish to acknowledge, with appreciation, the contribution of Advanta, which has helped to underwrite the cost of the exhibition. Last, and most emphatically, we express our deepest gratitude to Mr. and Mrs. Meyer P. Potamkin. Their enthusiasm and support for this project have been fundamental to its success. Like Louise and Walter Arensberg, Albert Gallatin, and Katherine Dreier, of the postwar period, Mr. and Mrs. Potamkin embody the ideal of the learned and discriminating collector, whose unabashed love for the art of "modern" times nourishes the most positive ideals of its underlying spirit.

Daniel Rosenfeld
The Edna S. Tuttleman Director of the Museum of American Art

Lenders to the Exhibition

Amon Carter Museum, Fort Worth, Texas
Mr. and Mrs. Irwin L. Bernstein
Birmingham Museum of Art, Birmingham, Alabama
The Brooklyn Museum, New York
CDS Gallery, New York
Columbus Museum of Art, Ohio
Denver Art Museum, Colorado
Margaret L. Driscoll
The Fine Arts Museums of San Francisco, California
Fisk University, Nashville, Tennessee
Georgia Museum of Art, University of Georgia, Athens
Hirshhorn Museum and Sculpture Garden, Smithsonian Institution, Washington, D.C.
Ellen Speiser Katz
Maurice and Margery Katz
Kennedy Galleries Inc., New York
Kraushaar Galleries, New York
The Metropolitan Museum of Art, New York
The Montclair Art Museum, New Jersey
Museum of American Art of the Pennsylvania Academy of the Fine Arts, Philadelphia
Museum of Fine Arts, Museum of New Mexico, Santa Fe
The Museum of Modern Art, New York
National Gallery of Art, Washington, D.C.
National Museum of American Art, Smithsonian Institution, Washington, D.C.
The Newark Museum, New Jersey
The Georgia O'Keeffe Foundation
Perry and June Ottenberg
Philadelphia Museum of Art, Pennsylvania
The Phillips Collection, Washington, D.C.
Mr. and Mrs. Meyer P. Potamkin
SBC Communications Inc., San Antonio, Texas
Mr. and Mrs. Philip Sherman
Temple University Libraries, Philadelphia, Pennsylvania
Whitney Museum of American Art, New York
Yale University Art Gallery, New Haven, Connecticut
Zabriskie Gallery, New York
Private collection

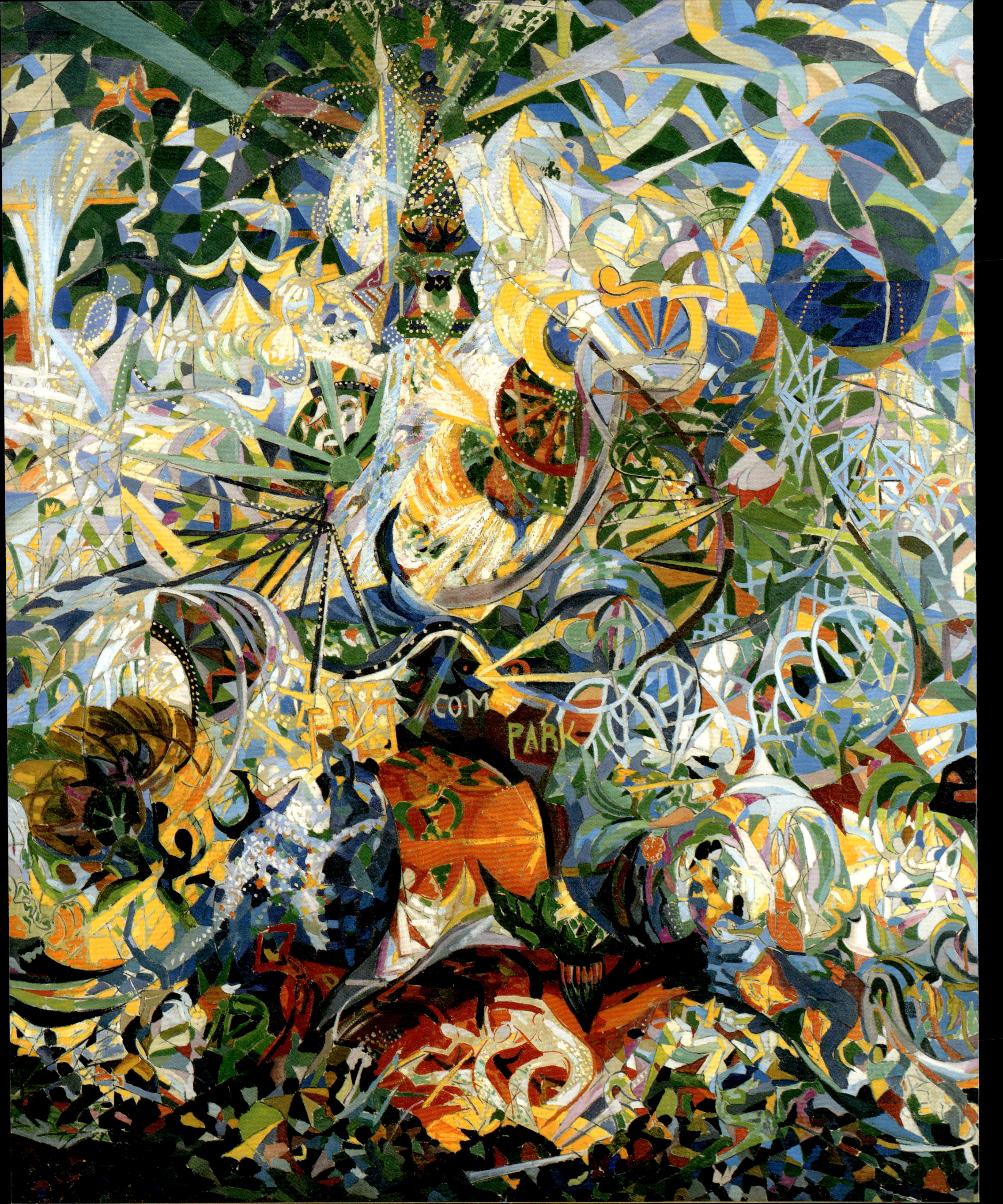
COM
PARK

ROCKING THE CRADLE OF LIBERTY:
PHILADELPHIA'S ADVENTURES IN MODERNISM

Sylvia Yount

"Modernism Invades Academy's Galleries!" . . . "Boredom Banished by the Modernists!" . . . "Jolt for Philadelphia!"[1] These were some of the colorful headlines that trumpeted the arrival of the "Exhibition of Paintings and Drawings Showing the Later Tendencies in Art." Held at the Pennsylvania Academy in the spring of 1921, it marked the first comprehensive display of American modernist works in an American museum. This essay explores a number of fundamental issues raised by the "Later Tendencies" effort, from the expansive definition of modernism in these years to Philadelphia's distinctive role in its popular acceptance. That the Academy laid the groundwork for such an enterprise—over at least two decades before the 1921 exhibition—also merits examination.

The title of the Museum of American Art's partial re-creation of this landmark show points up one of its central themes: what it meant "to be modern" to a generation of American artists at a particular time and place. "Modern" is a relative term, suggesting a commitment to contemporary life. Therefore, what is considered modern today may not be tomorrow, but remains in constant flux. It was in the first two decades of this century that the concept came to be seen as a style in both the visual and literary arts. As such, modernism was more of a cultural attitude than a coherent movement—an effort to turn away from the past and look to the future, to disparage the old and celebrate the new.

Joseph Stella's electrifying *Battle of Lights, Coney Island, Mardi Gras* (1913) [p. 59], one of the most acclaimed works in the "Later Tendencies" exhibition, in many ways codifies what we have come to think of as modern in cultural and artistic terms. Its rhythmic bursts of color and energy convey a subjective response to one popular dimension of urban consumerism, while its innovative composition and raucous abstraction lend visual expression to the transformative culture of the so-called Jazz Age.[2]

Aesthetically, the image reveals an American artist's debt to the European avant-garde—in Stella's case, his compatriots, the Italian futurists. (Stella was born in Italy but emigrated to New York at the age of nineteen, establishing his artistic career there.)[3] "To be modern" in America meant not only defying the rules of tradition, rules that were inherited from Europe, but also translating a new transatlantic language into a domestic idiom. Such a process leads us back to Philadelphia's Pennsylvania Academy of the Fine Arts, and to the seemingly oxymoronic discussion of modernist activities at a reputedly conservative institution.

Founded in 1805 on the model of Britain's Royal Academy, the Pennsylvania Academy was America's first museum and school of fine arts. In spite of this classical foundation, expressed in the school's traditional curricula and the museum's occasionally safe curatorial practice—from its earliest days in Frank Furness's extraordinary building (considered a masterwork of "modern" architecture when it

Joseph Stella
Detail: Battle of Lights, Coney Island, Mardi Gras
1913
Oil on canvas
75 ¾ x 84"
Yale University Art Gallery, Bequest of Dorothea Dreier to the Collection Société Anonyme

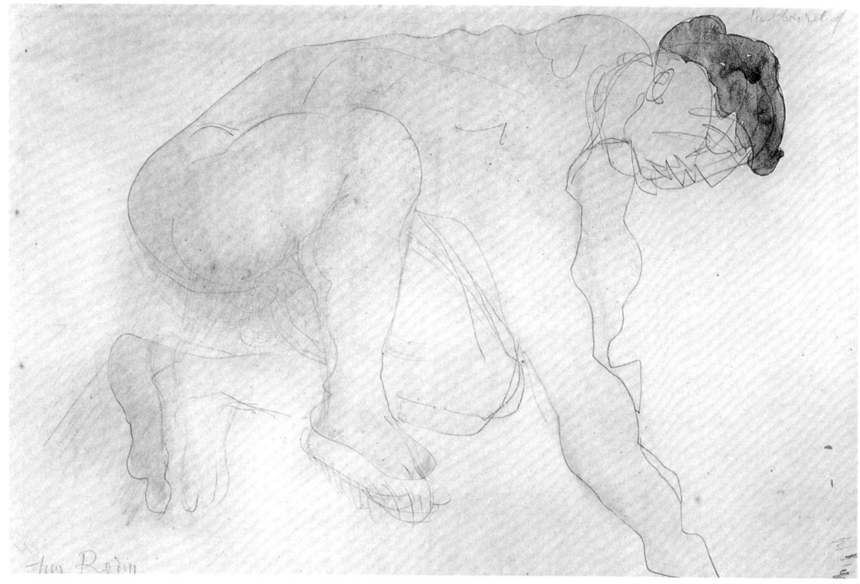

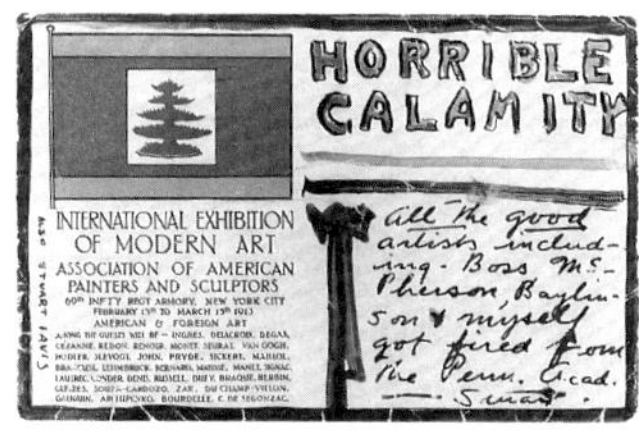

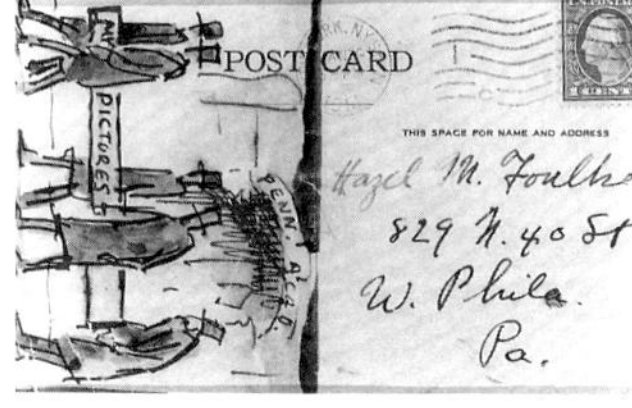

1. Auguste Rodin
Kneeling Male Nude
Ca. 1900
Pencil and watercolor on buff wove paper
7⅞ x 12¼"
Bequest of Jules E. Mastbaum; Rodin Museum, Philadelphia

2. Stuart Davis
Armory Show announcement
1913
Pen and ink on paper
Collection of Earl Davis

opened in 1876) through the twenties—the Academy earned a reputation as a modern art institution. In fact, the Philadelphia landmark boasted a far more progressive profile than its New York counterpart, the National Academy of Design.[4]

Much of this repute resulted from what was happening in the school—namely, Thomas Eakins's introduction and rigorous application of the French Ecole des Beaux Arts curriculum, which emphasized a thorough study of the human figure. Eakins was followed in the school in the 1890s by American impressionists like Robert Vonnoh and William Merritt Chase. Significantly, the institution was a great popularizer of impressionism; its support of the progressive style, through both faculty appointments and museum exhibitions, meant that while cultivating a taste for American impressionism among the general public, the Academy also trained young artists in its merits.

At the turn of the century, Thomas Anshutz (a protégé of Eakins who, later, had agitated for his dismissal) played a role in further defining the school's progressive character by encouraging the painterly expressions of Ashcan artists like John Sloan and William Glackens, as well as those of early modernists such as Arthur B. Carles, Charles Demuth, John Marin, Morton L. Schamberg, and Charles Sheeler, many of whom also studied with Chase. Thus, throughout its history, the Academy's school may be seen as having nurtured, sometimes in spite of itself, the avant-garde impulses of its student body.[5]

The special exhibitions held at the Academy were also key to this effort. In general, these shows were more reflective of the institution's progressive character than its annual juried exhibitions. The latter were intended to be representative of art being produced across the country and not just by a northeastern vanguard.[6]

In addition to granting early recognition to so-called secondary media such as etching, watercolor, and illustration (the first display of "fine art posters" in the country was held at the Academy), it was also the first American museum to promote photography as a fine art. A series of photographic salons in the 1880s and around the turn of the century introduced the Academy to an important modernist tastemaker, Alfred Stieglitz. The tie between Stieglitz and the Academy continued to be fruitful throughout the early decades of this century.

Further examples of the institution's innovative exhibition policy include the first American display of the sculptor Auguste Rodin's nude drawings, in 1905 [fig. 1], followed by another showing three years later of a larger selection.[7] Moreover, in 1908, the group of artists known as the Eight, who laid the groundwork for modernism in America with its landmark exhibition at the Macbeth Gallery, in New York, brought the show to the Academy shortly after.[8]

Yet, despite this progressive profile in Philadelphia, there were always students who characterized the Academy as out of touch with the contemporary art world. This charge heated up around 1913 with the advent of the "International Exhibition of Modern Art." Popularly known as the Armory Show because it was held at New York's 69th Regiment Armory, this watershed exhibition was America's first large-scale introduction to European and American modernism. Stuart Davis, an occasional Academy exhibitor, sent an amusing postcard to a Philadelphia cousin announcing the acceptance of his work in the show. Noting that "all the good artists . . . got fired from the Pennsylvania Academy," presumably because of a modernist association, Davis emphasized his perception of the institutional conservatism by sketching a vignette of pallbearers toting his work away from the Academy's hallowed arches [fig. 2].

Although Davis's playful posturing was not entirely groundless (the Academy's annual exhibitions, at this time, continued to feature the now-mainstream impressionists over younger, more experimental painters), much of the disparaging of the institution may be viewed as part of a natural cycle of youth rebelling against its elders. Indeed, many students actively pursued alternative sites for the display of their work in these years, focusing on a number of local commercial venues—from galleries to department stores—and artists' clubs.[9]

For example, in 1916, H. Lyman Saÿen and Morton Schamberg, two Academy alumni who, by this time, had established themselves as leading modernist figures, organized Philadelphia's "First Exhibition of Advanced Modern Art," at the McClees Galleries. A commercial space noted for its adventurous shows, the gallery had, a few years earlier, given Schamberg and his classmate Charles Sheeler their first solo exhibitions.[10] The 1916 effort featured a group of thirty-one, mainly European works drawn from the Armory Show, by artists whom the organizers considered second-generation modernists, including Matisse, Picasso, Duchamp, and Brancusi. As such, it marked the first major presentation of avant-garde art in Philadelphia.[11] One local journalist anticipated the effect of the show coming three years after the Armory event, which had been less than well received in the city.[12] "If the test of the pudding is the eating, the test of the modernists lies in the seeing of their works, not once but often."[13]

The critical response to the McClees show acknowledged the value of the organizers' didactic aims—to illustrate modern painters' transition from representation to a realm of sincere emotion—and applauded their open-minded selections. Helen Henderson, the *Philadelphia Inquirer*'s art critic with modernist sympathies, noted that the four-week exhibition demonstrated "how ready is the public to visit art exhibitions of a live and interesting character. The exhibition proved the most popular one ever held in this gallery, and attracted an unprecedented number of visitors."[14]

The popular success of Schamberg and Saÿen's effort revealed the existence of an audience for modernism in Philadelphia. Indeed, there are further indications that the city's appreciation of advanced art was nourished by a series of events at the Academy, long before the advent of the Armory Show. The Rodin example has already been cited. Furthermore, in the Academy-sponsored 1911 Water Color annual, John Marin exhibited fifteen of his recent works [fig. 3].[15] In that show—the Academy's earliest display of a body of work by the younger generation of graduates whose sojourns in Paris had encouraged avant-garde approaches to art-making—Marin's group of watercolors generated strong reactions. In language that was to typify many journalists' confused encounters with American modernism in future years, the *Philadelphia Public Ledger* voiced concern about "the freaks of the futurists and the secessionists," singling out Marin's work with a paraphrase of Rudyard Kipling: "It is not pretty, nor is it art."[16]

Other reviewers recognized, albeit with marked ambivalence, the significance of Marin's work for the course of American art in general:[17]

Wrong these things may be. They are far apart from anything that has been done in the past. It is doubtful whether anyone over forty in his heart of hearts will really admire them; but they drive home to their high purpose with a force which changes canon and convention and awakens unbounded enthusiasm in the student of today; the artist of tomorrow.[18]

Clearly, there were a few critics who sought to understand this new artistic language and make it intelligible to viewers. Helen Henderson [fig. 4], a former student of Anshutz and active member of the Fellowship (the Academy's alumni association), was one.[19] In addition to covering Philadelphia's modernist adventures for the *Inquirer*, she frequently reported on Stieglitz's activities at 291, the gallery that, by 1908, had become the leading venue for European and American modern art in the nation.

In the years following the Armory Show, a number of other private galleries dedicated to the promotion of modern art opened in New York. The Bourgeois, Carroll, Daniel, and Modern galleries featured the work of a diverse group of American artists, from members of the Eight to those associated with Stieglitz's circle, as well as European practitioners.[20] Significantly, Stieglitz closed 291 in 1915, leaving his colleague Marius de Zayas to seek commercial support for advanced art with the Modern Gallery. No longer the only tastemaker on the block, Stieglitz, nevertheless, continued to play a role in the promotion of avant-garde American art in the years before the 1925 opening of his

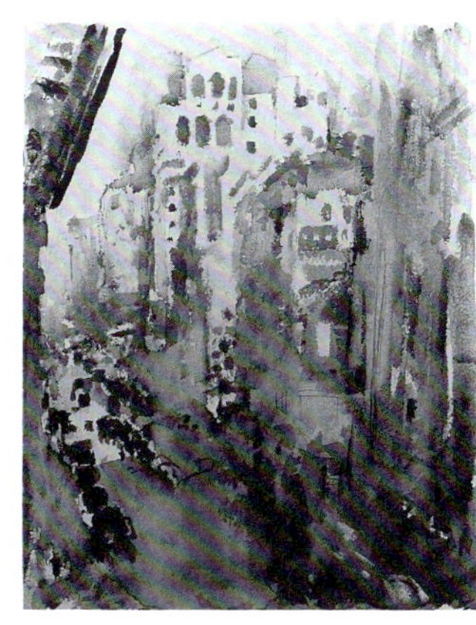

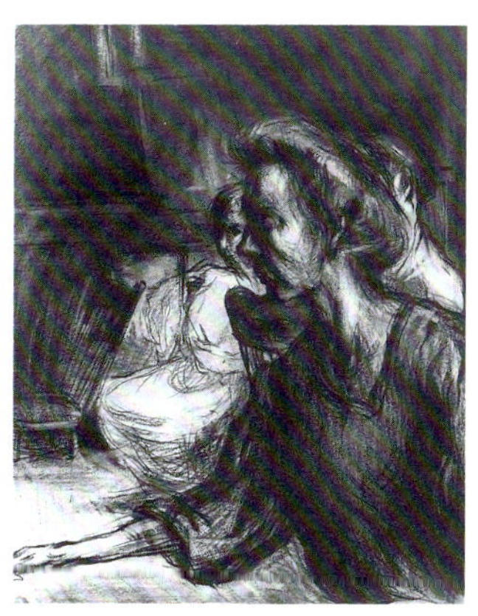

3. John Marin
From the Window of "291," Looking Down Fifth Avenue
1911
Watercolor and pencil on paper
16⅜ x 13⅜"
Lent by The Metropolitan Museum of Art, Alfred Stieglitz Collection, 1949

4. Charles Demuth
Helen Henderson
Ca. 1906
Charcoal, graphite, and ink on cream wove paper
9 13/16 x 7 13/16"
Museum of American Art of the Pennsylvania Academy of the Fine Arts. Academy Purchase, 1957.20

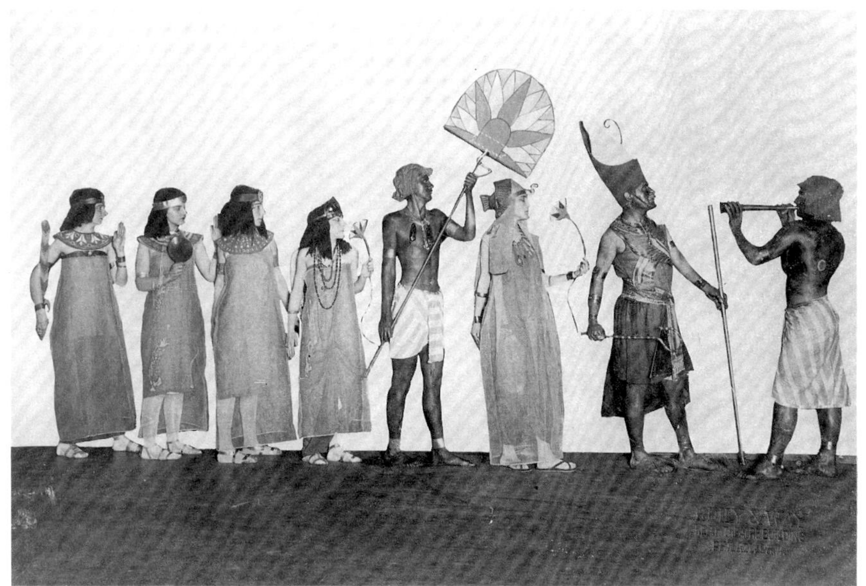

5. Unknown photographer

Egyptian Pantomime, "The Masque of the Primitive Peoples"

1915

Archives of the Pennsylvania Academy of the Fine Arts

next formal venture, the Intimate Gallery.[21] One of the institutions where he worked in the interim, on a somewhat freelance basis, was the Pennsylvania Academy.

Much had changed at the Academy in the years since Stieglitz's previous involvement with the photographic salons. In the school, Anshutz's death, in 1912, led to the hiring of two artists more closely associated with conservative practice—the Bostonian Philip Leslie Hale and a former Academy student, Daniel Garber. Nevertheless, there were other instructors, with direct ties to the Paris and New York worlds of the avant-garde, who continued to encourage individual expression in the student body, namely Hugh Breckenridge and Henry McCarter, themselves both Academy graduates.[22] In 1917, Arthur B. Carles, another former student, joined the faculty. After the untimely deaths of Saÿen and Schamberg, in 1918, Carles became the leading modernist spokesperson in Philadelphia.[23]

The activities of the Academy's three recognized modernists—Breckenridge, McCarter, and Carles—unquestionably contributed to the growing acceptance of progressive tendencies in the city and set the stage for the 1921 effort. Always conscious of their role as educators, they employed a variety of strategies to speed the popularization of modernism in its many cultural forms.

The post-Armory Show art market in Philadelphia was not as radically transformed as New York's—much of the modernist action continued to occur within the Academy's purview—but a broader avant-garde scene was on the rise. The English-born Leopold Stokowski had arrived in 1912 to conduct the Philadelphia Orchestra, encountering a formidable wall of musical conservatism. His efforts to educate the public in the merits of progressive composers like Schoenberg and Scriabin began to produce results by the beginning of the next decade. Soon thereafter, the Curtis Institute of Music and a variety of local dance companies were established, all part of Philadelphia's emerging "cultural renaissance." Weekly salons and musicales also brought a European sensibility to the Quaker city.[24]

According to the lawyer and modernist sympathizer R. Sturgis Ingersoll, music played a primary role in the development of Philadelphia's progressive culture:

> *It was not all paint. A great part of the general belief in the day came from the Orchestra. The Friday afternoon concert audience dispersed to teas and talk—the Saturday night audiences to hours of conversation . . . in houses up and down Walnut, Locust, Spruce, and Delancey Streets. . . . The painters, the musicians, the Museum people, and amateurs of one sort or another, mixed in a cheerful belief that something was happening.*[25]

Carles, McCarter, and Breckenridge all belonged to this larger circle of cultural activists, which tended to define its mission dramatically. At this time, according to the twenties' cultural historian Constance Rourke, American culture in its entirety—politics, religion, the arts—was pure theater.[26] This view of the postwar generation as the most theatrical to date is borne out by Philadelphia's modernists.

Throughout its history, Philadelphia had been an important dramatic center; by the turn of the century, it was second only to New York in its breadth of theaters. A number of artful spectacles in the teens positioned the Academy at the progressive center of this activity. In the bohemian tradition of art students' costume balls and amateur productions, a series of artists' masques—involving various local art institutions, but directed by an Academy representative—were held between 1915 and 1917.[27]

Arguably, the precedent for such local theatricals had been set by former student Robert Henri's Walnut Street studio burlesques of the 1890s.[28] These playful diversions led to the Academy's 1894 presentation of *Twillbe*, a parody of George du Maurier's popular novel of Parisian bohemia, *Trilby*. With Henri and three Ashcan artists—John Sloan, Everett Shinn, William Glackens—in leading roles, the production indirectly engendered numerous innovations in popular theater. It also revealed the close link between spectacle and "modern" culture that continued throughout the twenties.[29]

The first Artists' Masque, titled "The Masque of the Primitive Peoples," was held at Horticultural Hall, in Fairmount Park, on April 16, 1915. As noted in the program, it was "undertaken primarily to bring the members of the several Art Organizations of Philadelphia into closer contact with each other."[30] While the Academy was represented by its most progressive faction—the Fellowship, performing an "Egyptian Pantomime" [fig. 5]—the institution lent additional support through an honorary committee, which included established artists, like Emily Sartain, Cecilia Beaux, and Charles Grafly, as well as the "moderns" Breckenridge and McCarter. McCarter played an even more active role in the production as "Master of Color and Design"—that is, director.[31] In addition to assigning different scenes to the seven participating institutions, McCarter designed the costumes for the Fellowship. Extensively covered by the local press, the performance ended with a costume ball open to the entire Philadelphia cultural community.[32]

The following year's masque—"The Masque of Ariadne"—held at the Academy of Music on February 22, again featured a pagan theme, with the Fellowship enacting "The Triumph of Dionysos." This time, Carles was responsible for the scenery, designing seven stage sets on the subject of Theseus and the Minotaur. (Significantly, one year later, the Academy hired Carles as an instructor in drawing and painting; his Saturday morning Costume Sketch Class quickly became a favorite of students.)[33]

Although no photographs or sketches of Carles's designs are known to exist, the program for the 1916 masque sports a flapperlike woman in Greek costume on the cover [fig. 6], suggesting the increasingly "modern" look of the performances.[34] Furthermore, the scenario for the "solar drama," written by a University of Pennsylvania instructor, used colored lights rather than set changes to advance the narrative—a dramatic device that Carles must surely have responded to creatively.[35] The "colorful spectacle" was highly praised by local critics and declared a "marvelous success," both financially and aesthetically.[36]

The masques of 1915 and 1916 were essentially costume pageants in the tradition of tableaux vivants—performed by the Fellowship at the Academy from the 1890s through the turn of the century—but the 1917 production was something else entirely.[37] For the first time, the Academy joined the alliance of organizations as an eighth body, separate from the Fellowship. With this increased involvement came greater creative control.

First, the Academy's announcement for the scenario competition called for a "decorative rather than realistic" stage setting: "The backgrounds of the Russian Ballet, 'Sumurun,' Granville Barker's productions and those of the Washington Square Players are suggested as appropriate."[38] Two Academy modernists, Carl Newman and Saÿen, were the chosen designers, with Saÿen also serving as director of the production. His involvement, combined with a number of other factors, guaranteed that for the first time in its history, the masque would be linked explicitly to modernism.

The Academy's reference to the "Russian Ballet" in its competitive call suggested a desire to align its production with the avant-garde.[39] Sergei Diaghilev's Ballets Russes, founded in Paris in 1909, first performed in Philadelphia in the spring of 1916, but its presence was felt a year earlier in the galleries of the Academy: From November 7 to December 12, 1915, a large selection of Leon Bakst's costume and stage designs for the ballet [fig. 7] was exhibited in the Philadelphia Water Color Club's thirteenth annual at the museum. The works created such a sensation that the Academy sponsored "Bakst Day," to which it invited prominent actors and actresses, members of local organizations "interested in drama and the new stagecraft," as well as "leaders in the moving picture field," to view the designs and hear lectures on Bakst's life and work.[40]

All three Artists' Masques revealed the direct influence of Diaghilev's troupe, from a fascination with pagan cultures to an emphasis on music, sets, and costume, as integral, interpretative aspects of

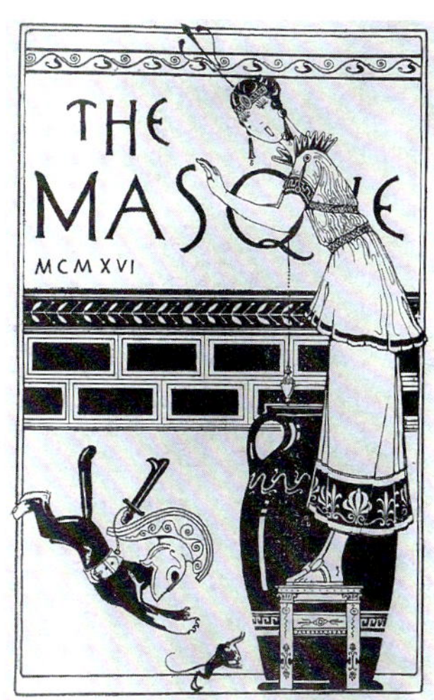

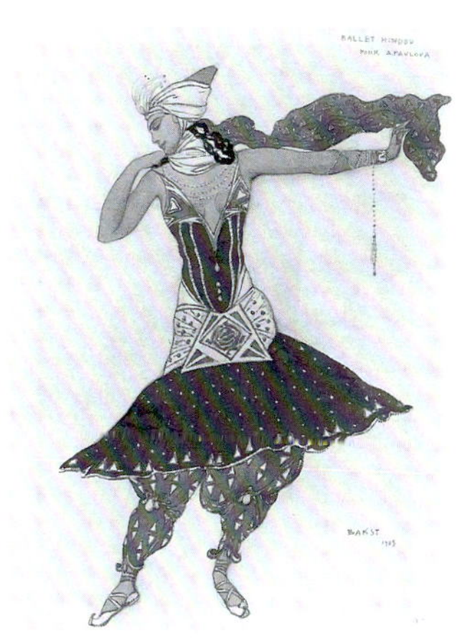

6. William M. Campbell
"The Masque of Ariadne" program cover
1916
Archives of the Pennsylvania Academy of the Fine Arts

7. Leon Bakst
Costume for Anna Pavlova
1913
Pencil and watercolor on white paper
12⅛ x 9⅛"
Isabella Stewart Gardner Museum, Boston

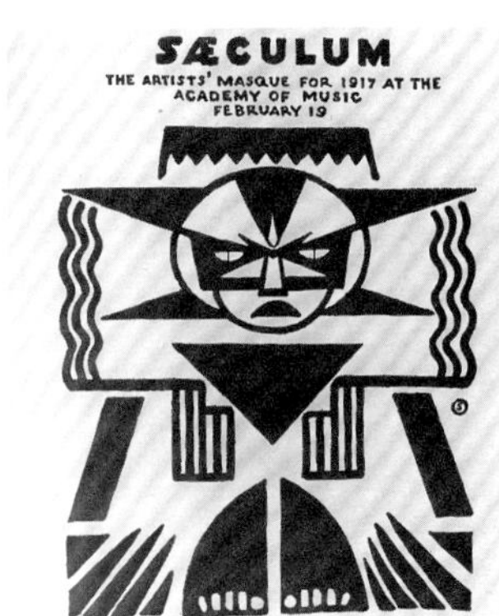

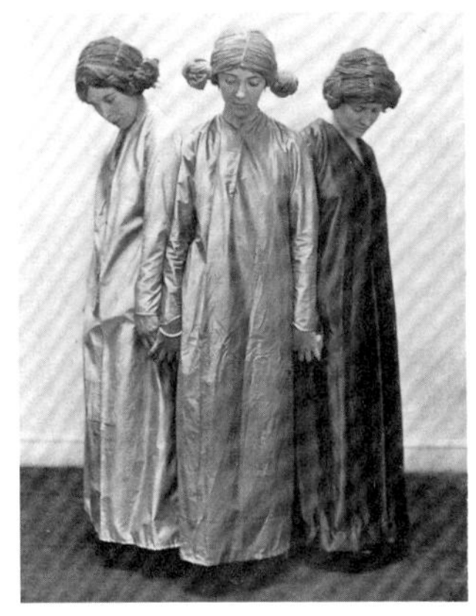

8. H. Lyman Saÿen
"Saeculum" program cover
1917
Archives of the Pennsylvania Academy of the Fine Arts

9. Unknown photographer
The Color Bearers, "Saeculum"
1917
Archives of the Pennsylvania Academy of the Fine Arts

the performance. Later referred to as "dynamic modernism," Diaghilev's aesthetic foregrounded the expressive significance of stagecraft as a means of fostering an audience's emotional response.[41]

The 1917 masque, titled "Saeculum [Eternity]," was described in the annual report of that year as embodying the "most modern movement in art." Accordingly, "an effort was made to render the abstract essence of the subject, and it was necessarily held together as a unit by one person, Lyman Saÿen, acting as director."[42] His capable hand also could be detected in the program's prospectus, from image [fig. 8] to text:

The Masque for 1917 will be presented in a new manner this year, in accordance with the most recent forms of plastic expression commonly known as "Modern Art.". . . It has been designed to live in the minds of those who witness its production with the calm yet active tranquillity which characterizes the arts of all times, and its particular method of presentation has never yet been used on any stage.[43]

Saÿen's description of the performance explicitly recalled Diaghilev's artistic goals:

The idea of the piece is expressed in terms which are to be understood emotionally, or in the spirit of pure decoration. In two prologues and two acts it will present the emotional episodes of the mental life in terms of dramatic action of the human form, color-forms, the spoken word, music and light; so arranged that these plastic elements aid each other by the law of contrast rather than harmony.[44]

The prizewinning scenario by William Albrecht Young, who had served as stage director for the two previous masques, called for a "color drama" between the Soul and the Cosmos.[45] The action of the performance, such as it was, derived from a synchronization of Saÿen's four "cubist" backdrops—depicting the atmospheric realms of the "Spirit of the Cosmos"—with Carl Newman's experimental costumes [fig. 9], as well as the lighting, music, and dance. As in 1915 and 1916, original music was composed by Herbert Muschamp; yet, the Japanese-inspired prologues, as well as the addition of "modern" incidental music by Debussy, Bizet, Rachmaninoff, and Glazunov, were a departure. As a highly esoteric aesthetic experiment, "Saeculum" literally defined the Academy's "modern spirit" by assigning the only spoken part in the production—"The Voice of the Spirit of the Cosmos"—to John Frederick Lewis, then president of the institution and vice-president of the Artists' Masque of Philadelphia's board of directors.

Somewhat surprisingly, "Saeculum" was considered a revelatory success of "artistic radicalism" by most local critics.[46] The performance also attracted the attention of Boston and New York papers, suggesting its recognized significance for the cause of the "new movement."[47] Reviewers noted the leading part Saÿen played, in both the conception and execution of the spectacle. A student of Matisse, Saÿen was one of the first Americans to fully understand and utilize the expressive fauvist approach to color:

Those of the modernists in art who rely on color, rather than form, to convey meaning and impressions, were given an opportunity to prove their case by means of the drama last night. . . . So far as the audience was concerned the case was proved.[48]

Another writer noted that the large, "bewildered" audience—held "spellbound for a few minutes as the performance ended"—may not have grasped the exact story of the masque, yet the "sheer conviction of the scene, the light, form and color," left viewers "with a desire to see it over and over again."[49]

Claiming that "Saeculum" shattered all rules of stagecraft, one critic detailed how the costumes and wigs—"of green, of scarlet, of orange, of red"—created brilliant effects when caught by the "colored rays from the spotlights and spectrums."[50] Another compared the spectacle to a huge canvas against which performers appeared as dabs of color. Undoubtedly, Saÿen was inspired by Diaghilev's treatment of the stage as a plastic space and his use of lighting, movement, and design to create volume.

Even more interesting, "Saeculum" recalled Wassily Kandinsky's scenario for a mixed-media spectacle, *The Yellow Sound*, published in the *Blaue Reiter* almanac of 1912. This culmination of Kandinsky's synesthetic fascination with interrelations among painting, music, and theater was never performed in his lifetime; however, the project may have been known to a select circle of Americans studying in Munich.[51] "Saeculum" also paralleled theories of the Italian futurists, published in a 1915 manifesto, and, most significantly, anticipated, by a few months, the landmark avant-garde ballet *Parade*. Performed by the Ballets Russes, with music by Satie, scenario by Cocteau, and designs by Picasso, *Parade* was heralded a "cubist manifesto" when it premiered, in Paris, in May 1917.[52]

While it is unlikely that Saÿen was familiar with either the futurists' writings or Picasso's sketches (having left Paris in 1914), and no direct link may be drawn between him and the *Blaue Reiter* group, his probable backdrops for "Saeculum" [fig. 10], as well as a number of his easel paintings at this time, do suggest the influence of Bakst and Matisse.[53] In this context, it seems wholly appropriate that the 1917 masque constituted Saÿen's last major work.

The vacuum created by the deaths of Saÿen and Schamberg, in 1918, coupled with Helen Henderson's departure from Philadelphia one year later, left the local modernist cause largely in the hands of such Academy associates as Carles, Breckenridge, and McCarter. The recent modernist convert and fellow alumnus William H. Yarrow also joined the effort.

Yarrow had come under the influence of Cézanne and, later, Stanton Macdonald-Wright during his time in Paris. Credited with being the only American modernist to establish a specific "school," Macdonald-Wright and his colleague Morgan Russell introduced their synchromist style to America in a 1914 exhibition at New York's Carroll Gallery. Drawn from late nineteenth-century color theories as well as a close study of Cézanne, synchromism stressed the primacy of color as a structural device and posited correspondences between music and painting.[54] After a series of successful exhibitions, in 1919 Macdonald-Wright disengaged himself from avant-garde activities in New York, moved to California, and, soon after, eschewed abstract painting.

The notion, embraced by critics at the time (as well as by some later art historians),[55] that 1919 witnessed, to a great extent, the "death" of modern art in America drew a lengthy retort from Yarrow, a response that established him as a new progressive voice in Philadelphia. Headlined as a "rebuke" to art critics and academicians who maintained that they had known since the time of the Armory Show that the "modern movement" would never amount to anything, Yarrow's newspaper feature highlighted many of the issues that were to define the modernist mission in the next decade.[56]

Ann Douglas has identified the twenties as a period of unprecedented collaboration between popular and elite culture, noting that artists maintained a belief that everything was "capable of popularization."[57] Indeed, a number of modernist organizations established at this time claimed as their primary objective the education of the critical and general public, in light of the relative success already achieved with many artists and connoisseurs. The Society of Independent Artists and the Société Anonyme, founded, respectively, in 1917 and 1920, were two such associations.

Established by a coalition of European and American artists, most of whom were associated with Louise and Walter Arensberg's avant-garde New York circle, the Society of Independent Artists was the first modernist organization to hold a continuing series of privately run exhibitions.[58] Its "no jury, no prizes" policy drew a wide variety of work that allowed the critics and general public to make their own aesthetic appraisal. This disinterestedness caused some reviewers to accuse the Independents of valuing quantity over quality; however, while the

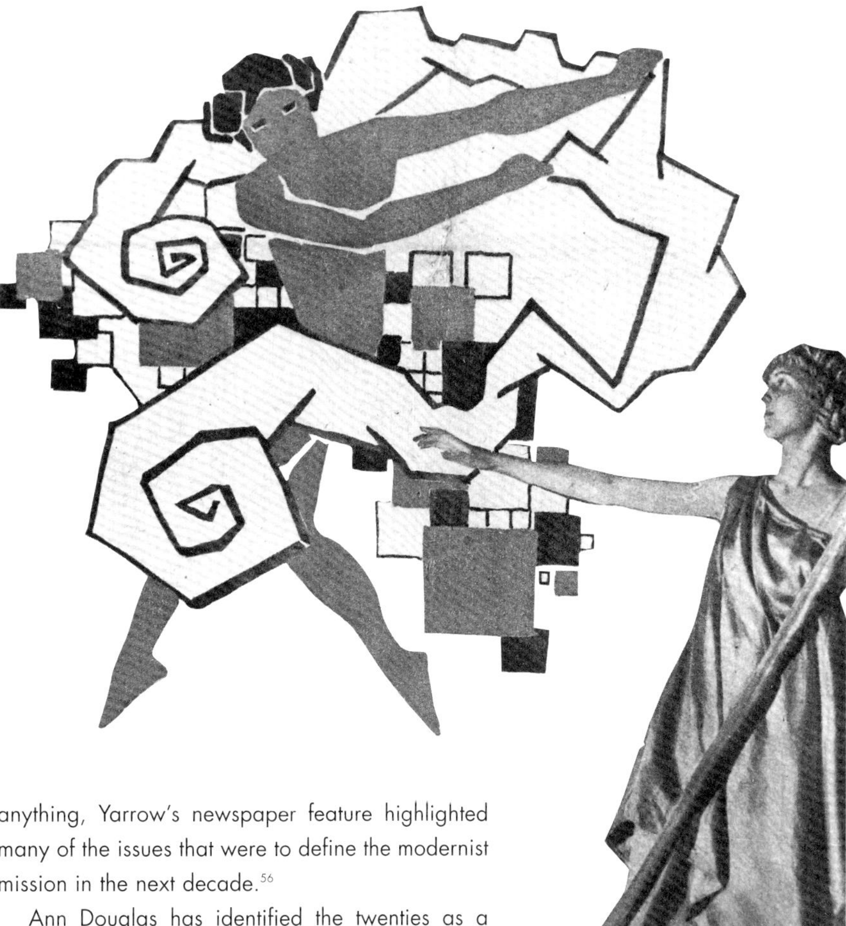

10. Attributed to H. Lyman Saÿen
"Saeculum" design
1917
Archives of the Plastic Club, Philadelphia

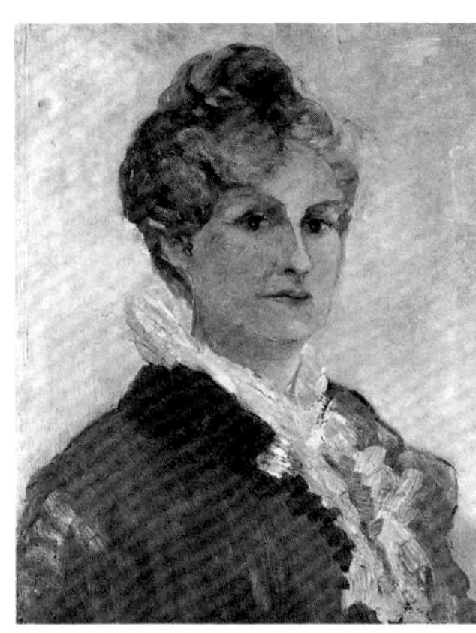

11. Katherine S. Dreier
Self-Portrait
1911
Oil on canvas
20 x 16″
Yale University Art Gallery, Bequest of Katherine S. Dreier to the Collection Société Anonyme

shows were often uneven, they attracted considerable attention and served as an important outlet for the exposure and development of taste for a broadly conceived modernism.

In 1920, three members of the Independents—Katherine Dreier [fig. 11], Marcel Duchamp, and Man Ray—joined forces to establish the Société Anonyme, America's first incorporated Museum of Modern Art. While the French name signaled the society's international character, Dreier's dual identity as a social activist and painter influenced its primary aim: to familiarize a broad American public with the most advanced art production, regardless of origin. In addition to holding exhibitions in its New York galleries, the organization sponsored public lectures and publications, and sent traveling shows across the country in an effort to publicize avant-garde art. What most distinguished Dreier's strategies was this emphasis on popular acceptance, a far cry from the elitism of such proselytizers and collectors as Stieglitz and John Quinn, who believed modern art could never be appreciated by the "masses."[59]

Post–Armory Show developments would seem to have made this type of campaign unnecessary, but World War I—the watershed of the decade—produced many changes in American culture that resonated in the arts. As the historian Lynn Dumenil has remarked, the refrain "since the war" was used by contemporaries to describe a spectrum of transformations in social values and institutions. Compared to Europe, America was left relatively unscathed by the conflict; yet, the Great War became a popular metaphor for understanding the nation's unsettled present and hopeful future.[60]

With Europe in ruins, America emerged from its 1917–18 involvement as an economic world power that, over the next decade, would seek cultural emancipation from the Old World.[61] The nation's dual strengths of democracy and plurality, which allowed for such prosperous conditions, both encouraged and complicated a growing political conservatism at home. The isolationist position that prevented the ratification of President Woodrow Wilson's League of Nations—an international effort to prevent future wars—also affected artistic life, as America turned inward with an eye to self-directed peace and prosperity. This cultural backlash and virulent nativism created a hostile environment for modern art, and dictated the intensification and refashioning of the American modernists' campaign.

The postwar ambivalence toward government and the increased incorporation of society also nourished a new cultural emphasis on individualism and self-expression. Rule-breaking, verging on what Douglas has called a "cultural activity," came to be seen as intrinsic to any form of artistic innovation.[62] In 1919, Yarrow chided critics who failed to understand the "absolute sincerity" and individuality of modern painters and could not discern their work as a logical step in the development of Western art:

The spirit that infuses the work of the "modernist" is the same that infuses all art, and has infused it through its tortuous path of evolution. It is nothing new, strange, nor grotesque, nor is it simply another sign of the general unrest that informs all present-day affairs, an unrest that is the expression of aesthetic freedom as well as social and political.[63]

In an effort to promote his point about the importance of interpreting modern art for the public, Yarrow soon joined with Carles and Carroll Tyson, a local artist and collector, in the organization of a special exhibition. "Paintings and Drawings by Representative Modern Masters," held in the spring of 1920, was the Academy's own particular version of the Armory Show and, appropriately, the first of three pioneering exhibitions of modern art that picked up where the Artists' Masques—discontinued because of the war—left off. Within three years, the large-scale spectacle of modernism in Philadelphia had moved from the stage into the galleries of the city's most venerable art institution.

Like the 1913 landmark, the "Modern Masters" exhibition functioned as a survey of modernist impulses in both historical and contemporary art. Unlike the Armory Show, however, the majority of the 254 works—paintings and works on paper—were European, loaned from such noted collectors as Stieglitz, Marius de Zayas, Lillie Bliss, and the Arensbergs, as well as a number of Philadelphians, including Earl Horter, Clement Newbold, and Tyson himself.[64]

Three works by James McNeill Whistler as well as forty-one paintings and prints by Mary Cassatt (the largest display of her work to date, primarily lent by her Philadelphia relatives) [fig. 12] were featured alongside other nineteenth-century luminaries, among them, Courbet, Degas, Manet, Monet, Renoir, Rodin, Toulouse-Lautrec, Gauguin, and Cézanne, the latter considered the "true 'master' of the 'Modernists.'"[65] Examples of the twentieth-century avant-garde included Matisse, Picasso, Braque, Severini, and Stanton Macdonald-Wright, one of only three Americans in the show. Such a highly diverse cast later led Stieglitz to declare the exhibition "a complete demonstration of the origin and development of the Modern Movement of Painting."[66]

Carles's intentions for the exhibition were primarily didactic and directed at students who had been "deprived of the opportunity of European travel and study the past five years of war, and even prevented by high railroad rates from frequent visits to the NY galleries."[67] Acting as curator, he installed the works in chronological order, setting the tone with the art of Whistler and Courbet and closing with Severini and Macdonald-Wright.

The organizers were also aware of the benefits of such a show in cultivating a broad public taste for modernism. By organizing the exhibition into a narrative of evolution versus revolution, Carles encouraged viewers to understand the more advanced work as a direct outgrowth of nineteenth-century experiments. The foreword to the catalogue, written by no less a local modernist than Leopold Stokowski, placed the burden of knowledge and taste squarely on the public's shoulders:

It is curious that while the music of Debussy, Strauss, Skryabin, Stravinsky, and Schoenberg is known and accepted in Philadelphia as of great aesthetic value, the paintings of Seurat, Renoir, Cézanne, Degas, Picasso and Matisse, outside of a few connoisseurs, are unknown or ridiculed.[68]

Adding that these artists have long been acknowledged in Europe as "masters," Stokowski called on Philadelphia to do the same:

It is important intrinsically, and also because a new school of painters is arising in America which is penetrating still farther in the direction taken by such masters as Cézanne, Picasso, and Matisse. It would be a great national loss if these should be unrecognized in their own country.[69]

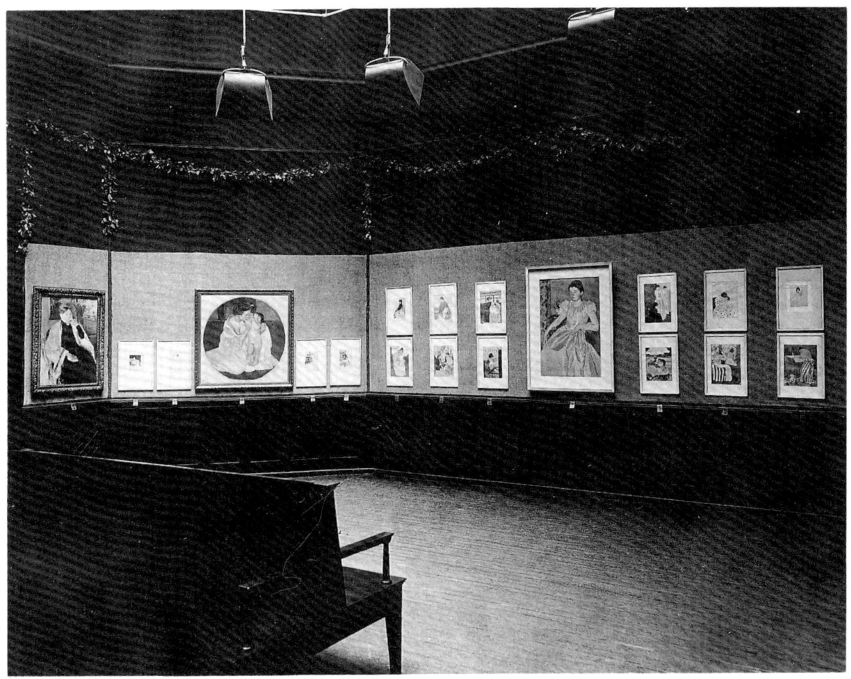

Critics and members of the general public apparently rose to the conductor's challenge. Indeed, during the exhibition's three-week run, it attracted more than twenty-five thousand visitors from around the country. Significantly, the "radicalism" of the show was largely identified with the unexpected host. Reviewers praised the Academy for its "unique" and "fascinating" special exhibition, noting,

Never before have the newer art tendencies been given official recognition at the Pennsylvania Academy of the Fine Arts. A too cautious conservatism has heretofore deprived Philadelphia of the opportunity of seeing for itself examples of the art which has excited derision and admiration and endless controversy the world over.[70]

As discussed earlier, the Academy, in fact, had been promoting modernism in various forms since 1905. "Modern Masters," however, was the museum's first special exhibition to feature a large collection of advanced painting, and the success of the effort was duly noted both inside and outside the institution.

One year later, the Academy took an even bolder step into the modernist arena with the "Exhibition of Paintings and Drawings Showing the Later Tendencies in Art."[71] This time, a selection committee of

12. Unknown photographer
Mary Cassatt installation, "Exhibition of Paintings and Drawings by Representative Modern Masters"
1920
Archives of the Pennsylvania Academy of the Fine Arts

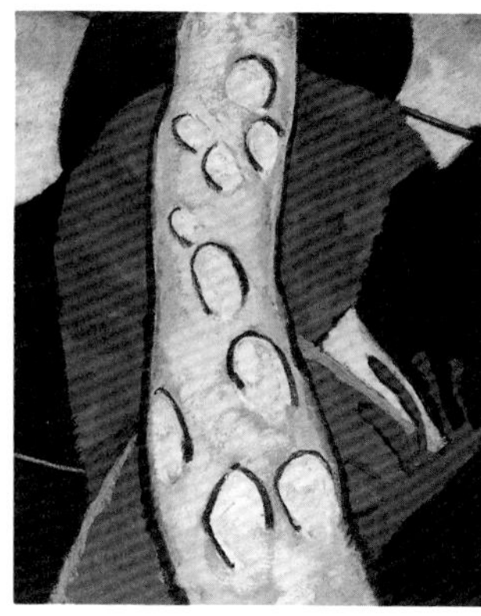

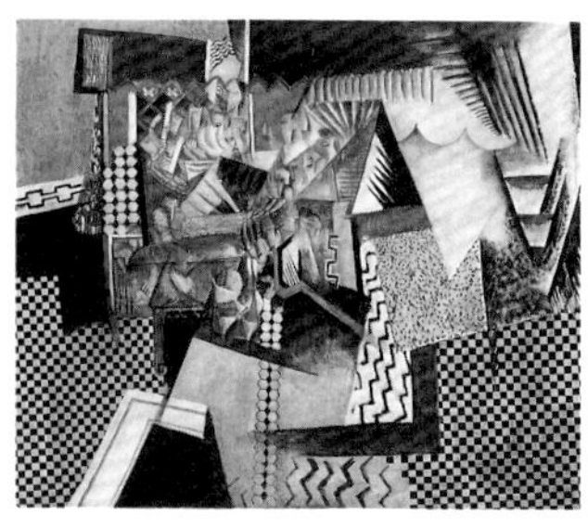

13. Arthur G. Dove
A Walk: Poplars
Ca. 1920
Pastel on silk mounted on board
21⅝ x 17⅞"
Daniel J. Terra Collection, 40.1982; Photograph ©1996 Courtesy of Terra Museum of American Art, Chicago

14. John Covert
Brass Band
1919
Oil and string on composition board
26 x 24"
Yale University Art Gallery, Gift of Collection Société Anonyme

15. Max Weber
Chinese Restaurant
1915
Oil on canvas
40 x 48"
Whitney Museum of American Art, Purchase

seven Philadelphia and New York artists was formed, with Yarrow at the helm.[72] Other members included Carles, Paul Burlin, and Bernard Gussow, as well as those with greater national reputations, then and now, like Thomas Hart Benton, Joseph Stella, and Stieglitz. Benton, Burlin, Carles, Stieglitz, and Yarrow also served on the hanging committee. The decision to employ a committee in the organization of the show was viewed as a corrective to the "no jury" policy of the Society of Independent Artists. Although careful not to refer to themselves as jurors, the members of the committee of selection intended to produce a more discriminating display of American modernism, thereby heading off the kind of criticism recently aimed at the uneven Independents' exhibitions.[73]

The inclusion of work by noted modernist tastemakers like de Zayas, Dreier, and Edward Steichen, as well as Stieglitz's involvement, surely encouraged the participation of major lenders, including the Philadelphians Martha and Maurice Speiser, as well as Charles Daniel, Ferdinand Howald, Agnes and Eugene Meyer, and John Quinn; Stieglitz also loaned many works from his personal collection. Such "official" sanction alerted both the public and press to the exhibition's significance.

The "Modern Masters" effort recalled the Armory Show, but "Later Tendencies" echoed the "*Forum* Exhibition of Modern American Painters." Held at New York's Anderson Galleries in the spring of 1916, the "*Forum* Exhibition" was conceived as a response to the Armory Show in its American, rather than European, focus and in its use of a selection committee to choose the "best" examples of modern art. The exhibition was organized by Willard Huntington Wright, art critic of the *Forum* magazine and brother of Stanton Macdonald-Wright, who enlisted the assistance of five figures from different sectors of the art world, including Stieglitz, Henri, and the critic Christian Brinton. The committee chose two hundred works by seventeen artists to present the broadest scope of American modernism to the public. Catalogue statements by artists and organizers furthered the exhibition's educational aims.[74]

Yarrow's conscious debt to the "*Forum* Exhibition" manifested itself in the 1921 show in another fundamental way: The selection of 280 paintings and works on paper (sculpture was excluded because of transport problems) by eighty-eight artists formed a coalition of modernist groups. Members of the Eight (Arthur B. Davies, William Glackens, John Sloan) who still worked in a primarily figurative, representational mode were paired with more avant-garde talents from Stieglitz's 291 stable (Charles Demuth, Arthur G. Dove [fig. 13], Marsden Hartley, John Marin, Georgia O'Keeffe), the Arensberg circle (John Covert [fig. 14], Man Ray, Charles Sheeler, Florine Stettheimer), and the Stein set (Arthur B. Carles, Alfred Maurer, Max Weber [fig. 15]). Indeed, the "Later Tendencies" show testified to the inclusive and incestuous richness of the modernist scene in New York and Philadelphia, and demonstrated that none of these "memberships" was mutually exclusive.[75]

The exhibition's carefully chosen title was key to the organizers' public intentions. Yarrow's emphasis on the plural tendencies conveyed the diversity of work to viewers, as it revealed the American modernists' hesitation to be limited by specific stylistic categories.[76] Certain critics, however, sought stronger moorings, identifying the Eight as "Post-Impressionists" or "moderns" and the more experimental artists as "Cubists" or "ultra-moderns." This categorization suggests that the various European styles were not clearly distinguished—or, for that matter, understood—by most American critics. Indeed, the variety of styles represented in the Academy's show reveals that, in 1921, the definition of modernism was still quite broad.[77]

The diversity of tendencies in the exhibition was closely paralleled by genre and subject matter.

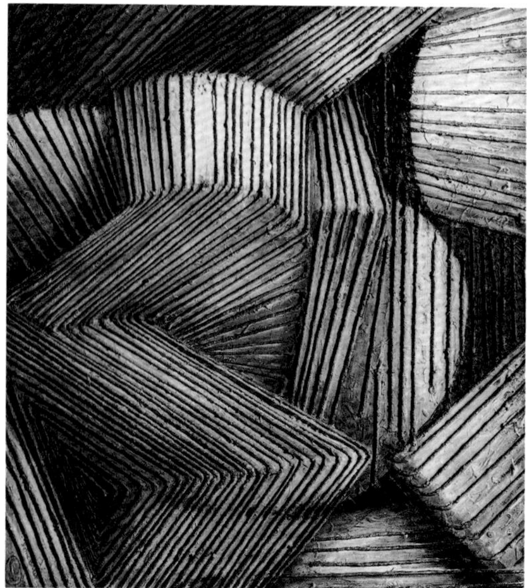

Although the influence of Cézanne and Matisse, among other European masters, was evident in a large portion of the work, a greater attention to native themes, unsurprising in the postwar era, asserted itself.[78] From an emphasis on the importance of place in urban and rural landscapes of New York, New Jersey, Maine, New Mexico, and California, and a celebration of consumer culture, to the primacy of the watercolor medium, which had come to be viewed as a distinctly national art form, the "Later Tendencies" exhibition aimed to present American modernism as a homegrown product, in both nostalgic and progressive terms.[79]

Interestingly, only one work in the "Later Tendencies" show explicitly referred to the Great War—Man Ray's *MCMXIV* (1914) [p. 54].[80] Florine Stettheimer's *A Day in West Point* (1917) [fig. 16] offered a more implicit reference to American military involvement, detailing an instance of personal patriotism. Stettheimer, whose American expatriate family had fled Europe at the outbreak of war, came to admire deeply her own country and value her "Americanness." Significantly, her other entry in the show, *Asbury Park South* (1920) [p. 60], depicting a segregated beach, was the only work to invoke the complex social tensions of twenties America.[81]

One of the most thoughtful reviews of the exhibition appeared in the *Dial*, the noted avant-garde journal that featured modernist imagery along with poetry, short stories, and critical features. In a piece titled "The Awakening of the Academy," published after the close of the exhibition, Thomas Craven commended the Pennsylvania Academy—to his mind, "one of the most conservative institutions in the United States"—for its "new vision." He also applauded the organizing committee for its "disinterested method of hanging the canvases, and for its inclusive choice of painters."[82]

Craven went on to discuss the show as a maturation of modernism that allowed the public, who had found a level of comfort with advanced work, to make "new valuations." Evidently, the organizers did not feel that the public needed the kind of critical guidance offered in the "*Forum* Exhibition" catalogue; no explanatory guidelines were offered in the checklist or on the gallery walls. (A facsimile of the 1921 checklist appears at the back of this catalogue.) Comparing the "Later Tendencies" show to the Independents' efforts in New York, Craven argued that "the future of American art will certainly repose in a number of men represented at Philadelphia, not in the illustrators, imitators, and literalists of fashionable exploitation"—implying that more of the latter were to be found in the New York exhibitions.

According to Craven, the greatest advance in the work of the modernists, as witnessed at the Academy, lay in the rejection of "experimentation" for its own sake and in the confident display of a breadth of individual expression. It was the latter that he viewed as the exhibition's distinctly "American" characteristic.[83] Craven concluded his article by noting that the Academy paid an "immense service" to modernism through this official recognition, thereby encouraging New York and Boston to "fall into line":

The life of art does not, of course, rest with the academies; but every exhibition increases the audience and encourages appreciation. In this manner the public would more quickly learn the value of the new men, and the dealer, whose interest in pictures is largely commercial, would be forced either to change his policy or to go out of business.[84]

That much of the art in the show had been produced a decade earlier and no longer provoked wild excitement in the public was, in the long run, beside the point. Highlighting the importance of creating a wider market for the work, Craven recognized that the organizers' primary aims were to demonstrate the appropriateness of modernism in the hallowed halls of the art museum. Philadelphia's precedent encouraged other American museums to feature advanced work, and 1921 marked a high-water mark in public acceptance. From the Société Anonyme's showings in Worcester, Massachusetts, and Brooklyn, New York, to Duncan Phillips's enterprise in Washington, D.C., modern art was being perceived as more accessible and not just the province of select collectors and aesthetes. This populist view of modernism coincided with the departure of a number of avant-garde players from New York, including the Arensbergs, who moved to California, and Man Ray and Duchamp, who returned to Paris.

Judging from the vast critical reception of the 1921 show, it was a success in the terms outlined

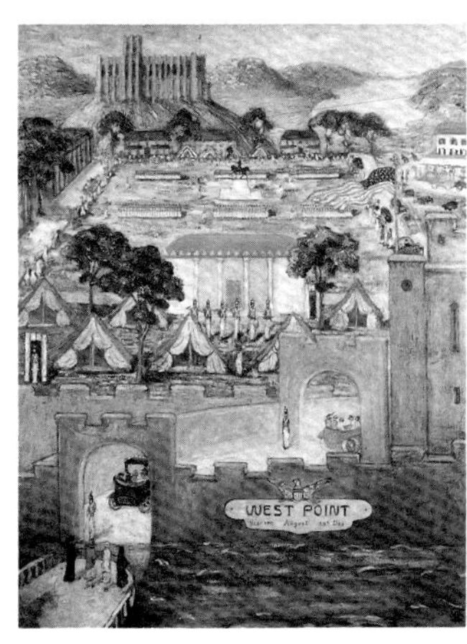

16. Florine Stettheimer
A Day in West Point
1917
Oil on canvas
Formerly The United States Military Academy, West Point
Present whereabouts unknown

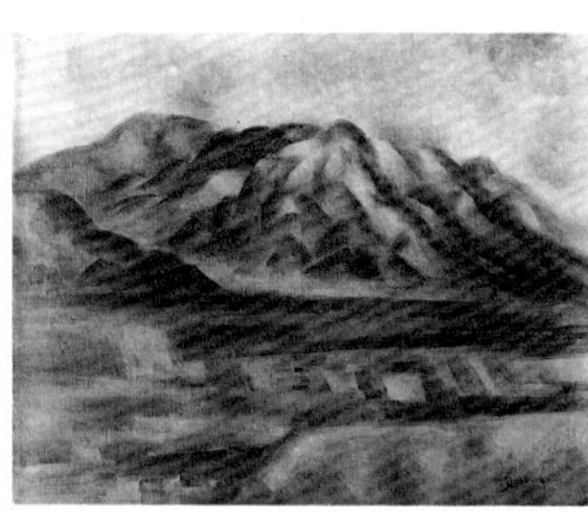

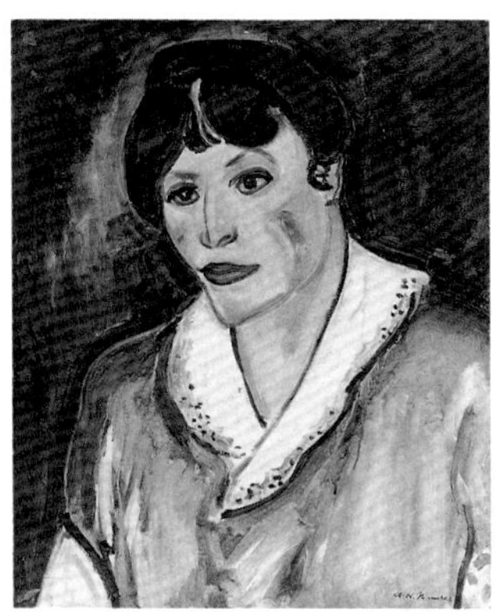

17. Andrew Dasburg
Landscape
Ca. 1920
Oil on canvas
Copyright ©1996 by
The Barnes Foundation

18. Alfred H. Maurer
Head: Number Three
Ca. 1906
Oil on canvas
Copyright ©1996 by
The Barnes Foundation

by Craven and the organizers. Although only a few works were sold from the exhibition—eight out of twelve to the noted local collector Albert C. Barnes [p. 36; figs. 17, 18]—it attracted large crowds and garnered many favorable reviews.[85] Two New York critics considered it the finest exhibition of modern American art ever held, noting that New York should have taken such a progressive step long ago.[86]

The theme of New York-Philadelphia competition ran throughout much of the commentary.[87] Although the *Dial*'s regular art critic, Henry McBride, declared at the beginning of 1921 that American art was "beginning to come into her own," and urged American artists to forego Paris for New York—"the centre of the universe"[88]—there is reason to believe that Philadelphia held competitive charms.

One New York reviewer noted that the Pennsylvania Academy "always has been more alive to the so-called 'moderns' than our [National] academy [of Design] has been"; another went further in drawing distinctions.[89] Comparing the exhibitions "Modern French Masters," at the Brooklyn Museum, and the upcoming "Impressionist and Post-Impressionist Painting," at the Metropolitan Museum of Art, with the "Later Tendencies" effort, the writer remarked of Philadelphia's Academy, "While New York and Brooklyn are coddling the French, the cradle of liberty will be rocked for the ultra-modernism of Young America."[90] This nationalistic rhetoric was employed more frequently after the war than before, when American modernists happily wore their European influence on their sleeves.

Newspaper coverage was just one indication of New York's recognition of this artistic "jolt for Philadelphia." For example, the Belmaison Galleries at Wanamaker's New York branch held a complementary exhibition, "Contemporary Painting and Sculpture," from April 25 to May 18. Referred to by one critic as "a small 'new tendencies' show . . . a little Academy of its sort, an amazingly complete affair," the Belmaison event included many of the same painters featured in Philadelphia, as well as some examples of sculpture and textile art (the latter by Marguerite Zorach).[91]

The Belmaison Galleries had opened in Wanamaker's New York store, in 1907, as the House Palatial, an experimental section of the furnishing and decoration department, featuring decorative arts.[92] An innovation of the founder's son Rodman, who became manager of the New York branch the same year, this "House of Ideas" began to display modern art—both European and American—in the late teens. Considering his Philadelphia connections and the department store's earlier promotion of modernism in the Quaker city, it is not surprising that Rodman Wanamaker would have coordinated an effort to further the goals of the "Later Tendencies" exhibition—that is, the popular acceptance of advanced art.[93]

Undoubtedly, this high profile of "Later Tendencies" resulted from a shrewd public-relations campaign, orchestrated by William Yarrow, months before the April 16 opening. One advance *Inquirer* notice warned that "all the reactionaries will have a splendid chance to wag their heads and murmur 'Tut-Tut' at this array of work, 'advanced,' we are told, to a point of utter radicalism."[94]

The critical consensus focused on the exhibition's "radical" nature, but one astute reviewer observed that the show would have dropped more of an "artistic bombshell" if it had occurred a decade earlier, and referred to it as "almost . . . a retrospective exhibition."[95] For a general public, however, the notion of modernism invading the Academy's galleries was startling.

Much of this conservative image of the institution derived from the nature of its annual exhibitions. The 1921 annual that preceded "Later Tendencies" by two months typified the Academy's contemporary

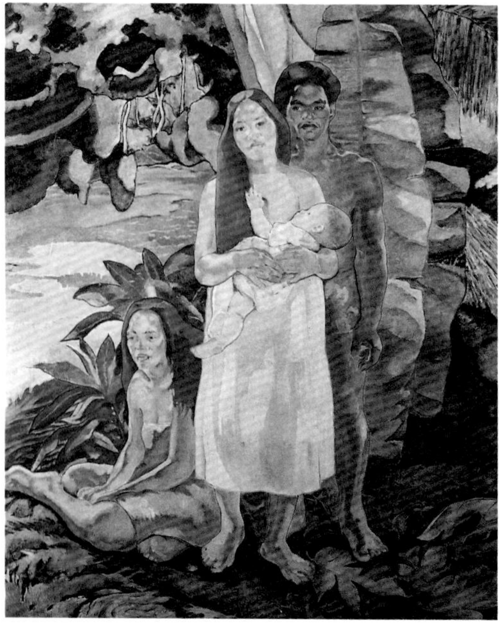

19. George Biddle
Tahitians
Ca. 1920
Oil on canvas
60 x 50 1/16"
Museum of American Art of the Pennsylvania Academy of the Fine Arts. John Lambert Fund, 1928.3

taste. Although a number of artists included in the annual also appeared in the modernist show—George Biddle, Arthur B. Davies, William Glackens, Gaston Lachaise, Henry McCarter, John Sloan—the prizewinning *Nude: Girl Combing Her Hair* (ca. 1920), a slick academic work by William McGregor Paxton, attracted the greatest public attention.[96] Museum purchases from the 1921 annual ranged from postimpressionist and Ashcan scenes to the Gauguinesque *Tahitians* (ca. 1920), by Biddle [fig. 19].

The newspaper coverage, as opposed to the generally more specialized art-journal reception, of the "Later Tendencies" exhibition revealed much about current public attitudes to modern art. As had been the case with both the Armory Show and the first Independents' exhibition, cartoons—a form of popular communication that surfaced around the turn of the century—were used to poke fun at the so-called radical vision and to undermine the seriousness of the modernist "cult."[97] By the twenties, as popular fads—from flagpole-sitting to crossword puzzles—permeated American culture, many viewers were quick to dismiss modern art as just another fashion, despite its apparent longevity. Moreover, modernism easily fell into the larger cultural discourse concerning "suckers" and "racketeers," a suspect component of urban consumerism in which "con games were culture."[98]

This notion of tricksterism and deception appeared in the negative responses to the Academy's show, a viewpoint ranging from the playful, as suggested by a *Public Ledger* feature [fig. 20] that smirked at the "extremist art pictures" and invoked Rudyard Kipling's famous phrase—"It's pretty, but is it Art?"—to the vitriolic.[99] The New York writer Alice Avon declared that the "later tendencies in art" were, in reality, "the most atrocious deficiencies and abnormalities."[100] The curious intensity of Avon's attack bears quoting at length:

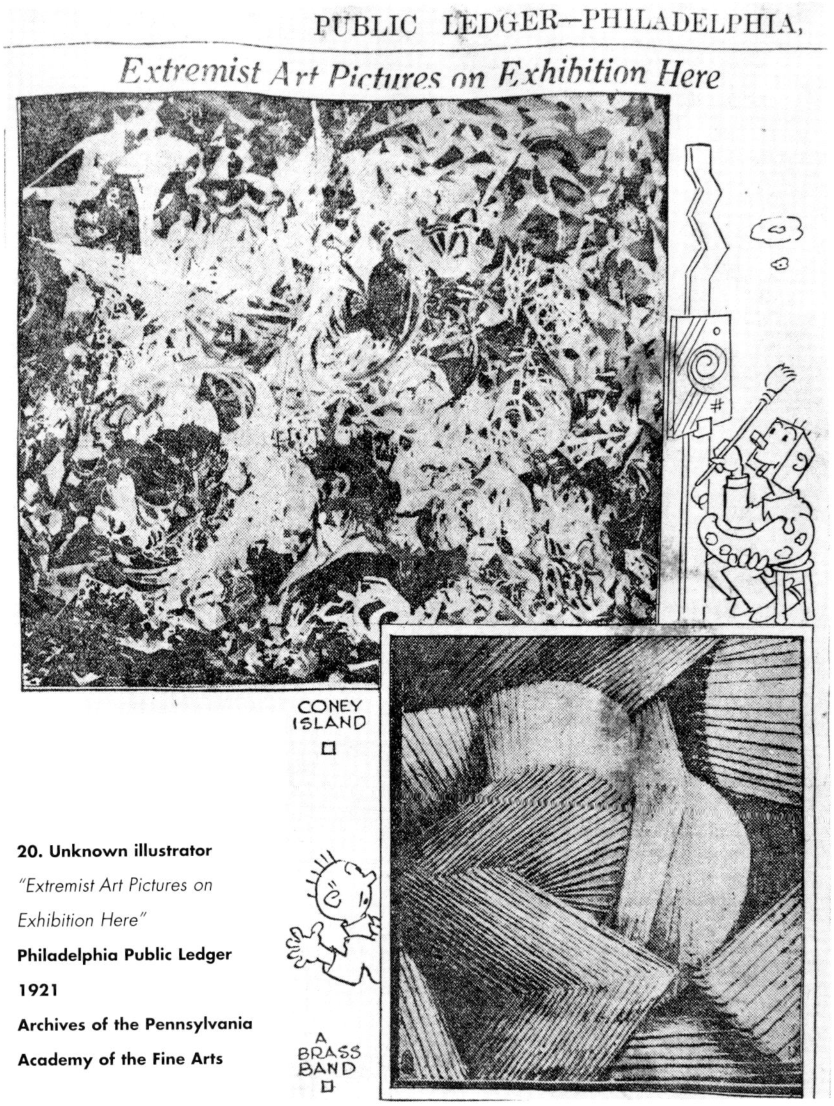

> *Instead of declaring in their advance publicity that "Philadelphia is establishing a precedent in the history of art by opening its door liberally to the radicals," it would be more appropriate to announce "Philadelphia leads the way in opening up the Chamber of Horrors" . . . for from every canvas shrieks loudly, "I am in the last stages of insanity." Then your hand wanders instinctively to your pocket to see if your gun is in position, in case one of the maniacs who gave vent to these crude despicable expressions is at large. You can believe me when I say that there is no green cheese or delicatessen supper that will ever make you dream such violent things as these.*[101]

PUBLIC LEDGER—PHILADELPHIA,

Extremist Art Pictures on Exhibition Here

CONEY ISLAND

A BRASS BAND

20. Unknown illustrator
"Extremist Art Pictures on Exhibition Here"
Philadelphia Public Ledger
1921
Archives of the Pennsylvania Academy of the Fine Arts

The association of madness with modernism—"art that looks crazy on display"—was a common trope in these years.[102] Indeed, a group of local alienists—that is, psychiatrists and neurologists—delivered a series of spring lectures at the Philadelphia Art Alliance in an attempt to discredit the Academy exhibition. In papers titled "The Abnormal in Art" and "The Evils of False Art," the specialists deemed it "a humbug exhibit with imbeciles, children, and ignoramuses as the principal exhibitors." One argued that certain "lopsided effects" of works on view indicated that the artists must have ghastly diseases of the mind, and that others, whose works were mere splashes of color and lines, were suffering from "color blindness and nearsightedness."[103] A few months later, this same group attacked the Metropolitan's display of French modernism, leading Albert Barnes to counter the charges with an offer to leave his vast art collection to the City of Philadelphia if any of the physicians could "prove himself qualified in the science of normal and abnormal psychology."[104]

Meanwhile, Barnes's high praise for the "Later Tendencies" show, which he saw as the "first real move to shake Philadelphia out of the lethargy which has been the reproach to us from artists and collectors of other cities," led directly to the Academy's third and final significant foray into modernist territory.[105] The 1923 special exhibition, "Contemporary European Paintings and Sculpture," largely organized by Carles and McCarter, featured recent additions to Barnes's private collection, never before seen in America.[106] Seventy-five works representing the most radical strain of European modernism, including Lipschitz, Modigliani, Soutine, Kisling, Derain, Picasso, and Matisse, were showcased in the museum's galleries and explained to the public through Barnes's five-page essay in the exhibition checklist.[107]

Evidently, the collector's commentary failed to sway either popular or critical opinion, and the general response to the exhibition ranged from bad to worse. Soutine's expressionist paintings particularly outraged local critics who had been sympathetic to the Academy's 1920 and 1921 special exhibitions of modern art. The consensus was most clearly articulated by Dorothy Grafly, who posited, "It is as if the room were infested with some infectious scourge." In fact, Grafly admitted that she preferred the Academy's collection of Peale portraits to the "modern horrors."[108] Barnes responded furiously to this display of "philistinism," packed up his art—vowing never again to show his collection in public—and retreated to the suburban-Philadelphia sanctuary of the Barnes Foundation.[109]

The negative response to the 1923 exhibition also adversely affected the Academy, scaring off the board from presenting any further exhibitions of modern art until the fifties, save for Breckenridge and McCarter retrospectives, in 1934 and 1943, respectively.[110] Turning its attention to the humanistic work of regionalists and social realists, along with the majority of America's art establishment (including earlier "moderns" like Benton), the Academy reclaimed its more conservative mantle.

This retrenchment was noted by no less a figure than Stieglitz, who, in 1936, sent a letter to the secretary of the Academy regretting the rejection from the annual exhibition of a Maine scene by Marin, one of Stieglitz's favorite artists. In a tone simply oozing with sarcasm, Stieglitz wrote:

> *I want to congratulate you on the qualifications of your Jury of Selection. Whoever the gentlemen (or ladies), they must all be fine artists. With Marin not up to their standard, your exhibition should be* the art event of the year! *Wake up ye Philadelphians.*[111]

Yet, the distance that the Academy traveled from Stuart Davis's disdain of 1913 to Stieglitz's of 1936 clearly involved a number of important detours in the development of modernist knowledge and taste. As the editor of the *Arts* magazine queried in September 1921, in response to another scathing letter of Stieglitz's, regarding the long-overdue display of French modernism at the Metropolitan, "Was there never a time, my dear Stieglitz, when you also were quite befuddled by 'modern art?' We all live and learn."[112]

Notes

1. See *Philadelphia Record,* April 9, 1921, *Philadelphia Inquirer,* April 16, 1921, and unidentified clipping; William Yarrow clipping file, Library of the Pennsylvania Academy of the Fine Arts.

2. For a creative, incisive study of the era's culture, see Ann Douglas, *Terrible Honesty: Mongrel Manhattan in the 1920s* (New York: Farrar, Straus & Giroux, 1995).

3. See Barbara Haskell, *Joseph Stella* (New York: Whitney Museum of American Art, 1994).

4. The Academy's highly progressive character between 1892 and 1905 can be linked directly to the presence of Harrison Morris as managing director. For a fascinating, albeit self-interested, account of life at the Academy in these years, see Harrison Morris, *Confessions in Art* (New York: Sears Publishing Company, 1930).

5. See Doreen Bolger, "The Education of the American Artist," in *In This Academy: The Pennsylvania Academy of the Fine Arts, 1805–1976* (Philadelphia: Pennsylvania Academy of the Fine Arts, 1976), 51–74.

6. For a comprehensive history of the Academy's annuals, see Cheryl Leibold's introductory essays in the three-volume *Annual Exhibition Record of the Pennsylvania Academy of the Fine Arts* (Madison, Conn.: Sound View Press, 1989).

7. The Academy's 1905 display of three Rodin drawings occurred at the annual exhibition of the Fellowship, the institution's alumni association. The prospectus for the exhibition stressed that it was "before all else an Artists' Exhibition . . . intended primarily for works which, by reason of their breadth of treatment or independence of ideas, would not be entered in the usual Exhibition." The Fellowship Committee at the time included "progressives" like Anshutz, Carroll S. Tyson, Alexander Stirling Calder, Robert Henri, and Henry McCarter. See *Sixth Annual Exhibition/Fellowship of the Pennsylvania Academy of the Fine Arts* prospectus; Archives of the Pennsylvania Academy. The 1908 showing of forty-six more Rodin drawings was part of the Philadelphia Water Color Club's sixth annual exhibition, cosponsored by the Academy. See the exhibition catalogues, Archives of the Pennsylvania Academy.

Stieglitz first exhibited Rodin's drawings in a January 1908 exhibition at the Little Galleries of the Photo-Secession, popularly known as "291," a reference to its Fifth Avenue address. See William Inness Homer, *Avant-Garde Painting and Sculpture in America, 1910–25* (Wilmington, Del.: Delaware Art Museum, 1975), 13.

8. An important discussion of the Academy's progressive activities can be found in Wilford Wildes Scott, "The Artistic Vanguard in Philadelphia, 1905–1920" (Ph.D. diss., University of Delaware, 1983).

9. Ibid., 155, 177. Scott cites Gimbel's and Wanamaker's as two local department stores that opened their galleries to European and American modern art in the teens. The Fellowship also provided outlets—sponsoring lectures in defense of modern art and including it in their annual exhibitions, which were held in the Academy's galleries. Furthermore, Philadelphia's Sketch Club frequently exhibited the work of local modernists; see 181, 188–90, 193.

10. James McClees's establishment was located at 1411 Walnut Street, opposite the Bellevue-Stratford Hotel, in the center of the city. Sheeler had his first solo show there in 1908, Schamberg in 1910. In 1917 and 1923, the gallery hosted exhibitions of the 31, a group of Academy students associated with Carles, Henry McCarter, and Hugh Breckenridge; see Barbara A. Wolanin, *Arthur B. Carles: Painting with Color* (Philadelphia: Pennsylvania Academy of the Fine Arts, 1983), 82, and "31 Artists Show Work at McClees,'" *Philadelphia Press,* April 15, 1917; Pennsylvania Academy of the Fine Arts scrapbooks, Archives of American Art, Smithsonian Institution, roll P56, frames 486, 489.

11. As Schamberg explained in the preface of the catalogue, "To serious students of the past hundred years in the history of painting, the various stages in its progress appear gradual, normal, and logical. Cézanne, Renoir, Seurat, Rousseau, Van Gogh and Gaugin [*sic*] have already taken their places among the old masters together with Delacroix, Courbet and Daumier." The represented Americans, besides Sayen and Schamberg, included Henry L. McFee, Walter Pach, Man Ray, Charles Sheeler, Joseph Stella, and Max Weber; see Scott, "Artistic Vanguard," 193–97, 221–22.

12. Ibid., 156–66.

13. Ibid., 195.

14. Ibid., 196–97.

15. In 1904, the Academy began segregating the annual display of works on paper in separate exhibitions. Just as this component of the annuals had previously been organized by the Philadelphia Water Color Club, the new watercolor exhibitions also became its responsibility. Drawing strength from the Academy's cosponsorship, which included a use of the museum's galleries and publicity machine, the club's annuals, in return, lent a decidedly progressive character to the establishment. The presence of Academy faculty known for their modernist sympathies also shaped the quality of the shows. Hugh Breckenridge, who served on the jury of selection for the 1908 annual that featured Rodin's drawings, was a member of the hanging committee in 1911. The 1911 jury of selection, which included McCarter and Anshutz, also chose a number of "advanced" European works by Kollwitz, Manet, Rops, Steinlen, and Toulouse-Lautrec. See the exhibition catalogues, Archives of the Pennsylvania Academy.

16. Quoted in Scott, "Artistic Vanguard," 120. The implied Kipling reference reads, "When the flush of a new-born sun fell first on Eden's green and gold, Our father Adam sat under the Tree and scratched with a stick in the mould; And the first rude sketch that the world has seen was joy to his mighty heart, Till the Devil whispered behind the leaves, 'It's pretty, but is it Art?'" See "The Conundrum of the Workshops" (1890), in *Rudyard Kipling's Verse, Inclusive Edition, 1885–1926* (New York: Doubleday, Doran and Company, 1931), 388–90.

17. For the issue of Marin's "modern" popularity, see Elizabeth Hutton Turner, *In the American Grain: Dove, Hartley, Marin, O'Keeffe, and Stieglitz—The Stieglitz Circle at The Phillips Collection* (Washington, D.C.: Counterpoint, 1995), 18–22, 34–38; and Jonathan Weinberg, "Why Marin?," *Block Points: The Annual Journal and Report of the Mary and Leigh Block Gallery, Northwestern University* 1 (1993): 20–33.

18. "Art and Artists," *Philadelphia Press,* November 12, 1911; quoted in Scott, "Artistic Vanguard," 120.

19. Henderson served as secretary of the Fellowship at the time of the first Rodin display. In 1911, she produced a historical study of the Academy—*The Pennsylvania Academy of the Fine Arts and Other Collections of Philadelphia*—lovingly inscribed and dedicated to Anshutz; Archives of the Pennsylvania Academy.

20. Judith Zilczer notes that between 1913 and 1918, thirty-four New York galleries and artists' organizations held more than two hundred fifty exhibitions of European and American modernism. See Zilczer, "The Armory Show and Its Aftermath," in *The Advent of Modernism: Post-Impressionism and North American Art, 1900–1918* (Atlanta, Ga.: High Museum of Art, 1986), 30–34.

21. See Turner, *American Grain,* 9–14.

22. Scott notes that this relationship between an academic institution and the avant-garde artistic sector was unique in America; see "Artistic Vanguard," 243.

23. An early devotee of Gertrude and Leo Stein's French avant-garde circle, Carles became one of the Academy's most charismatic and popular teachers, in large part because of the Parisian air he brought to the studio. See *Pennsylvania Academy Moderns, 1910–1940* (Washington, D.C.: National Collection of Fine Arts/Smithsonian Institution Press, 1975), and Abraham Davidson, *Early American Modernist Painting, 1910–1935* (1981; New York: Da Capo Press, 1994), 229–45.

24. For Stokowski and "modern" music in Philadelphia, see Nathaniel Burt, *The Perennial Philadelphians: The Anatomy of an American Aristocracy* (Boston: Little, Brown and Company, 1963), 471–76. Also see Wolanin, *Carles,* 69–70. For a discussion of modernist literary activities centered around the University of Pennsylvania, see Robert M. Crunden, *American Salons: Encounters with European Modernism, 1885–1917* (New York: Oxford University Press, 1993), 83–101.

25. R. Sturgis Ingersoll, *Henry McCarter* (Cambridge, Mass.: Riverside Press, 1944), 75.

26. See Douglas, *Terrible Honesty,* 55.

27. I am grateful to Cheryl Leibold, archivist of the Pennsylvania Academy, for sharing her research on the masques. For a discussion of similar entertainments in New York, see Steven Watson, *Strange Bedfellows: The First American Avant-Garde* (New York: Abbeville Press, 1991), 228–31, 320–24.

28. See Bennard B. Perlman, *Painters of the Ashcan School: The Immortal Eight* (New York: Dover Publications, 1979), 47–50.

29. In 1912, Shinn founded the first "little theater" in Greenwich Village. His company, the Waverly Place Players, performed burlesque melodramas, some of which were later incorporated into national vaudeville acts. See Sylvia Yount, "Consuming Drama: Everett Shinn and the Spectacular City," *American Art* 6 (Fall 1992): 102. For a discussion of other little-theater groups, like the Washington Square Players and the Provincetown Players, see Watson, *Strange Bedfellows,* 212–24.

In 1915, Morton Schamberg produced set designs for the initial "cubist" production in America. The Philadelphia Stage Society, the city's first little-theater group, commissioned the artist to produce a backdrop for an "eccentric" drama set in Spain—Richard Beamish's *Three Women.* See Kenneth Macgowan, *The Theatre of Tomorrow* (New York: Boni and Liveright, 1921), 117.

30. The other organizations included the Philadelphia Sketch Club, the Pennsylvania Museum and School of Industrial Art, the Philadelphia School of Design for Women, the T-Square Club, the Plastic Club, and the Art Club. Interestingly, Wanamaker's department store once again aligned itself with a "modern" venture, providing the only advertisements in the program. See *The Masque of the Primitive Peoples,* Archives of the Pennsylvania Academy.

31. 1915 saw McCarter turning away from the art of illustration to painting. His friendships with Sayen and Carles, as well as his experiences in Paris, shaped his modernist beliefs. One year later, he delivered a talk on "Ancient and Modern Art" at the Academy, in which he traced modern abstraction to various cultures' deep-rooted knowledge of design. See Archives of the Pennsylvania Academy.

32. "Artists in Delightful Show," *Philadelphia Evening Bulletin,* April 7, 1915; Pennsylvania Academy scrapbooks, Archives of American Art, roll P56, frame 253.

33. A greater seriousness toward the masques is noted from the August 1916 Act of Incorporation, which called for "an annual, or more or less frequent, ball, masque, fantasy, show, pageant or dancing assembly . . . offering an opportunity for the application of art knowledge to practical ends in the materialization of artistic conception"; Archives of the Pennsylvania Academy. See also Wolanin, *Carles,* 61–63.

34. The 1916 honorary committee added the likes of Thomas Eakins and Charles H. Stephens to its earlier core. Because of Eakins's ongoing progressive reputation in the city, despite his rather conservative artistic production, his presence must have been symbolic. A former student of Eakins, Stephens recently had distinguished himself as one of the more creative residents of the local Arts and Crafts community, Rose Valley. Along with his wife, Alice Barber, another successful student of Eakins, Stephens had organized a series of theatricals at the community's Guild Hall. See Ann Barton Brown, "'Joy is not Joy that is not Shared'—Life in Rose Valley," in *A Poor Sort of Heaven, A Good Sort of Earth: The Rose Valley Arts and Crafts Experiment* (Chadds Ford, Pa.: Brandywine River Museum, 1983), 87–91.

35. See "Artistic Masque Seen by Enchanted Crowd," *Philadelphia Record*, February 23, 1916; Pennsylvania Academy scrapbooks, Archives of American Art, roll P56, frame 241. Wolanin describes how the study of music and color occupied many Philadelphians in these years. For instance, in the early twenties, the noted modernist collectors Martha and Maurice Speiser commissioned the Clavilux, a "color organ" that coordinated chromatics of light and sound; see *Carles*, 63, 70. It was publicly exhibited at Wanamaker's in 1922, and later used by Stokowski in the film *Fantasia*.

36. See "Artists Romp in Gorgeous Pageant," *Philadelphia Press*, February 23, 1916; Pennsylvania Academy scrapbooks, Archives of American Art, roll P56, frame 240. In light of the masque's success, Harrison Morris proposed that the city send the show on the road, to cities like New York, Chicago, and Boston, in an effort to "advertise Philadelphia." Morris argued that the "Masque of 1916" revealed, in an entertaining and educational manner, what the city could do in the area of applied arts. See "The Masque of 1916," *Philadelphia Public Ledger*, February 26, 1916; Pennsylvania Academy scrapbooks, Archives of American Art, roll P56, frame 240.

37. For a brief discussion of tableaux at the Academy, see Cheryl Leibold, "Photographic High Jinks at the Pennsylvania Academy of the Fine Arts," *Nineteenth Century* 12 (1993): 2–7. Scott refers to the 1917 masque as "the most comprehensive statement of modern esthetics to be presented in Philadelphia"; "Artistic Vanguard," 197.

38. Archives of the Pennsylvania Academy. For modernist theater groups, see Kenneth Macgowan and William Melnitz, *The Living Stage: A History of the World Theater* (Englewood Cliffs, N.J.: Prentice-Hall, 1955).

39. The Ballets Russes toured Europe between 1910 and 1913, influencing advanced literature, theater, design, fashion, and painting. Indeed, the modernist painter Florine Stettheimer was deeply affected by a performance of Diaghilev's *L'Après-midi d'un faune*—danced by Nijinsky, with sets by Leon Bakst—which she saw in 1912. She later designed her own ballet, *Orphée of the Quat'z Arts*, based on the Parisian masques. Barbara Bloemink argues that all of Stettheimer's work from this time on bears the influence of the Ballets Russes. See Bloemink, "Visualizing Sight: Florine Stettheimer and Temporal Modernism," in *Florine Stettheimer: Manhattan Fantastica* (New York: Whitney Museum of American Art, 1995), 74–77.

40. "Bakst Day at Arts Academy," *Philadelphia Press*, November 14, 1915; Pennsylvania Academy scrapbooks, Archives of American Art, roll P56, frame 329. That many of the designs were to be worn by the Ballets Russes in its performance at Philadelphia's Metropolitan Opera House a few months later was an added draw. See "Thespians at 'Bakst Day,'" *Philadelphia Telegraph*, November 16, 1915; roll P56, frame 331.

41. See Bloemink, "Visualizing Sight," 74.

42. *Annual Report of the Pennsylvania Academy of the Fine Arts* (1917), 10; Archives of the Pennsylvania Academy.

43. *Saeculum* prospectus; Archives of the Pennsylvania Academy.

44. Ibid.

45. For a discussion of Young's initial, even more radical scenario, see Macgowan, *Theatre of Tomorrow*, 117; "Artists' Masque Drives To Absinthe," *Philadelphia Evening Ledger*, February 20, 1917; Plastic Club scrapbooks, Archives of American Art, roll 2537, frame 257.

46. See "Artists in Masque of Bizarre Beauty," *Philadelphia Inquirer*, February 20, 1917, and "Masque a Big Success," *Philadelphia Record*, February 20, 1917; Pennsylvania Academy scrapbooks, Archives of American Art, roll P56, frame 472.

47. See Scott, "Artistic Vanguard," 224.

48. "Saeculum, Art Masque, Is Carnival of Color," *North American*, February 20, 1917; Pennsylvania Academy scrapbooks, Archives of American Art, roll P56, frame 473.

49. Ibid., "Masque of Bizarre Beauty," *Philadelphia Inquirer*, and "Wonders of 'Saeculum' Still Being Discussed," *Philadelphia Press*, February 21, 1917; Plastic Club scrapbooks.

50. "Masque a Big Success," *Philadelphia Record*.

51. Marsden Hartley came under Kandinsky's influence between 1912 and 1915; see Gail Levin, "Marsden Hartley, Kandinsky, and *Der Blaue Reiter*," *Arts Magazine* 52 (November 1977): 156–60. See also *The Yellow Sound* program, The Solomon R. Guggenheim Museum, 1982. The spectacle premiered at the Guggenheim during the "Kandinsky in Munich, 1896–1914" exhibition. I am grateful to Cheryl Leibold for alerting me to the Kandinsky precedent.

52. Bloemink, "Visualizing Sight," 74. For a discussion of Enrico Prampolini's *Manifesto for the Futurist Stage*, see Scott, "Artistic Vanguard," 225. For *Parade*, see Patrick O'Brian, *Pablo Ruiz Picasso: A Biography* (New York: G. P. Putnam's Sons, 1976), 217–26.

53. For example, see his *Decor Slav* (ca. 1915) and *The Thundershower* (1917–18), both in the collection of the National Museum of American Art, Smithsonian Institution. One critic noted the relationship of the later work to Saÿen's contemporary masque backdrops and other design projects—namely, the spectrum of radiating colors he had painted on the studio ceiling of his friend and collaborator Newman. See Adelyn D. Breeskin, *H. Lyman Saÿen* (Washington, D.C.: National Collection of Fine Arts/Smithsonian Institution Press, 1970), 27.

54. See Melvin P. Lader, Wilford Scott, and Patrick L. Stewart, "The Synchromists," in Homer, *Avant-Garde Painting and Sculpture in America, 1910–25*, 20–21. The theory of correspondence was closely related to synesthesia, a term describing a sensory stimulation that causes another sense to respond. A popular literary and visual device of the turn-of-the-century avant-garde, its American adherents included Stieglitz, Georgia O'Keeffe, and Arthur Dove. See Charles C. Eldredge, *Georgia O'Keeffe: American and Modern* (New Haven and London: Yale University Press, 1993), 168–70.

55. See Scott, "Artistic Vanguard," and Patrick Stewart and Gilbert Vincent, "Changing Patterns in the Avant-Garde: 1917–25," in Homer, *Avant-Garde Painting and Sculpture in America, 1910–25*, 27–28.

56. William H. Yarrow, "A Painter Rebukes the Art Critics and Academicians," *Philadelphia Press*, May 18, 1919, section 4:14.

57. Douglas, *Terrible Honesty*, 69–70.

58. The exhibitions were held annually in New York from 1917 to 1944; see Roberta Tarbell, "The Society of Independent Artists," in Homer, *Avant-Garde Painting and Sculpture in America, 1910–25*, 25. For a comprehensive study of the Arensberg circle, see Francis M. Naumann, *New York Dada, 1915–23* (New York: Harry N. Abrams, 1994).

59. In 1923, the Société sent a selection of work to the Michigan State Fair; Stewart and Vincent, "Changing Patterns," 28. See also Naumann, *New York Dada*, 155–61, and Ann Temkin, "Brancusi and His American Collectors," in *Constantin Brancusi, 1876–1957* (Philadelphia: Philadelphia Museum of Art, 1995), 55–56.

60. See Lynn Dumenil, *The Modern Temper: American Culture and Society in the 1920s* (New York: Hill and Wang, 1995), 10–11, and Douglas, *Terrible Honesty*, 181–82.

61. Douglas notes that while the war set back the European economy eight years, it advanced America's by six; *Terrible Honesty*, 182.

62. Ibid., 481.

63. According to Yarrow, a series of negative reviews of the Society of Independent Artists' 1919 exhibition at the Waldorf-Astoria, in New York, occasioned his response; see "A Painter Rebukes." In the same issue of the *Press*, Yarnall Abbott outlined the "merry war" between New York critics and artists that resulted from the show; "Comment on Art, Artists and Their Work," *Philadelphia Press*, 6.

64. In discussing the exhibition, Ingersoll noted that local holdings of nineteenth-century French art were formed under the "tutelage" of Mary Cassatt. He credited Tyson with securing the Cézannes from New York and Philadelphia collections; see Ingersoll, *McCarter*, 72–73. For a discussion of the lack of cooperation from noted Philadelphia collectors of "modern" art, most likely Barnes, see "Modern Artists Represented in Noteworthy Exhibition," *Philadelphia Press*, April 18, 1920; Pennsylvania Academy scrapbooks, Archives of American Art, roll P56, frame 683. The show caused one reviewer to urge Philadelphia to make efforts to secure the collections before they were "sold to other cities." See "Philadelphia Is Warned To Save Its Art," *Philadelphia Inquirer*, April 18, 1921; Pennsylvania Academy scrapbooks, Archives of American Art, roll P56, frame 683.

65. James B. Townsend, "Modern Art in Philadelphia," *American Art News* 18 (May 8, 1920): 3. Manet's *Olympia* and Gauguin's *Ia Orana Maria* were just two of the more well-known works in the exhibition.

66. Alfred Stieglitz, "Regarding the Modern French Masters Exhibition, A Letter," *Brooklyn Museum Quarterly* 8 (July 1921): 107–8. Perhaps a sign of lingering animosity, no German artists were included in this postwar exhibition; van Gogh was another curious omission. As a whole, the exhibition revealed Philadelphia's overtly French-modernist leanings.

67. See Townsend, "Modern Art in Philadelphia." One local critic commended Carles and Tyson for attempting such a major loan show—a "mental and physical strain in these days of railroad strikes and difficulties of freight communication"—and declared their historical installation "brilliant." See "Radical Art at the Academy," *Philadelphia Public Ledger*, April 18, 1920; Pennsylvania Academy scrapbooks, Archives of American Art, roll P56, frame 682. Another noted that the show had drawn art students and schoolchildren from throughout the city, as well as from Wilmington and Trenton. See "Fine Arts Exhibit To End; Is Success," *Philadelphia Inquirer*, May 9, 1920; Pennsylvania Academy scrapbooks, Archives of American Art, roll P56, frame 685.

68. See *Catalogue of an Exhibition of Paintings and Drawings by Representative Modern Masters* (1920), 4; Archives of the Pennsylvania Academy.

69. Ibid.

70. Albert Sterner, "Modern Art Has Its Day at the Pennsylvania Academy," *Philadelphia Press Sunday Magazine*, Summer 1920.

71. As with earlier Fellowship and Water Color annuals, the Academy opted to lend its galleries to the show with "courtesy," rather than act as sole sponsor. For Yarrow's regret at this decision, see his letter to John Andrew Myers, March 7, 1921; Archives of the Pennsylvania Academy. Although the Academy did not provide its letterhead for the exhibition announcement, the press and public credited the institution with setting a precedent in the display of American modernism.

72. Yarrow's letters to John Frederick Lewis, the Academy's president, trace the evolution of the show, from its original conception as a group exhibition of "four men" to the "general exhibition" that resulted. At the request of the Academy, he presented a petition of twenty-six artists—"the younger generation of painters, to whom new means of expression and a personal viewpoint are paramount"—and convinced the board that such an exhibition would attract the very best "modern" work. See Archives of the Pennsylvania Academy.

73. One writer viewed this effort as an "academization of the moderns," but welcomed the "discipline and crystallization that Philadelphia will give the exhibition . . . a sort of 'now or never' importance." See "Modernism Academizes," *American Art News*, n.d.; William Yarrow clipping file, Library of the Pennsylvania Academy.

74. Yarrow, who published a book on Robert Henri in 1921, would have been very familiar with the *Forum* precedent. See William M. S. Rasmussen, "The *Forum* Exhibition," in Homer, *Avant-Garde Painting and Sculpture in America, 1910–25*, 24–25.

75. In simple terms, the 1921 roster was nearly identical to that of the Society of Independent Artists, save for European representation. Glackens, who served as president of the Society in its first year of existence, was followed by Sloan one year later. Other officers included Arensberg, Covert, Marin, Man Ray, Schamberg, and Stella; see Tarbell, "Independent Artists," 25. For a useful chart of these concentric artistic circles, see Watson, *Strange Bedfellows*, 392–95.

76. See Yarrow's March 7 letter to Myers, in which he suggested changing the name of the exhibition from "latest Tendency" to "later Tendencies," noting its more "elastic" meaning; see Archives of the Pennsylvania Academy. "Tendencies" was a popular term at the time and used in various studies; see Lorada Taft, *Modern Tendencies in Sculpture* (Chicago: University of Chicago Press, 1921).

77. A decade later, modern art came to mean solely abstraction rather than representation, and numerous "moderns," including Benton, Hartley, and Macdonald-Wright, identified themselves as "regionalists." For this recent appraisal of Hartley's career in the thirties and forties, see Donna M. Cassidy, "'On the Subject of Nativeness': Marsden Hartley and New England Regionalism," *Winterthur Portfolio* 29 (Winter 1994): 227–45.

78. Interestingly, the "Later Tendencies" exhibit overlapped at the Academy with a display of Swiss paintings, one of Christian Brinton's efforts to promote "national modernism." For more on Brinton's international ventures, see Andrew Walker, "Exhibiting Nationalism: Christian Brinton, Modernism, and the Construction of National Identity, 1910–1935" (Ph.D. diss., University of Pennsylvania, forthcoming).

79. For the "native soil" argument, with Albert Pinkham Ryder marking the genesis of American expression in paint, see Paul Rosenfeld, "American Painting," *Dial* 71 (December 1921): 649–70. For a discussion of watercolor as inherently "American" and "modern," see Marilyn Kushner, *The Modernist Tradition in American Watercolors, 1911–1939* (Evanston, Ill.: Mary and Leigh Block Gallery, Northwestern University, 1991), and Carol Troyen, "A War Waged on Paper: Watercolor and Modern Art in America," in *Awash in Color: Homer, Sargent, and the Great American Watercolor* (Boston: Museum of Fine Arts/Bulfinch Press, 1993), 35–74. McBride noted, in May 1921, "We are beating the world in watercolors, just now"; quoted in Troyen, 35.

80. Even though one commentator noted in a review of the Academy's 1921 annual that "the painter, like the novelist, deems it prudent to ignore the war in choosing subjects"—Gertrude Vanderbilt Whitney's sculpture, *Honorably Discharged*, was the only explicitly war-related submission—a special exhibition of war portraits followed the annual exhibition and preceded the "Later Tendencies" show. See "Another Academy Exhibition," *Philadelphia Inquirer*, February 7, 1921; Pennsylvania Academy scrapbooks, Archives of American Art, roll P56, frame 713.

81. See Dumenil, *Modern Temper*, 201–49. For Stettheimer's involvement with black culture, see Linda Nochlin, "Florine Stettheimer: Rococo Subversive," in *Stettheimer*, 105–6.

82. Thomas Jewell Craven, "The Awakening of the Academy," *Dial* 70 (June 1921): 673–78. See Dorothy Grafly's similar assessment of the exhibition, "Freaks in New Art Justified by Their Vogue, Says Critic," *North American*, April 17, 1921; William Yarrow clipping file, Library of the Pennsylvania Academy.

83. After outlining eight "tendencies" in the show, Craven admitted that such classification was reductive as they all overlapped; "Awakening of the Academy," 677.

84. Ibid., 678.

85. Barnes's purchases numbered Thomas Hart Benton, *The Beach* and *Study for Decoration*; Louis Bouché, *East and West*; Andrew Dasburg, *Landscape*; James A. Daugherty, *Hands of Moses*; Bernard Gussow, *Landscape*; Alfred Maurer, *Head: Number Three*; and Maurice Sterne, *Taos Indian Woman*. Earl Horter bought Joseph Stella's *Waterlilies*, the Speisers selected Benton's *Landscape*, and Alexander Lieberman purchased Marion Beckett's *Tiger Lilies* and Preston Dickinson's *Landscape: Number Two*. See Pennsylvania Academy Sales Book, 1921 entries; Archives of the Pennsylvania Academy.

86. See Peyton Boswell, "Philadelphia Sees Best in New," *American Art News* 19 (April 23, 1921): 6; Forbes Watson, "Comment on the Arts," *Arts* 1 (May 1921): 34; and "Philadelphia Leads the Way," undated, unidentified clipping; William Yarrow clipping file, Library of the Pennsylvania Academy.

87. Albert Barnes noted the great number of "out-of-town artists, critics, and collectors . . . the New York crowd" that the show brought to the Academy. See "Expert Praises Modern Show," *Philadelphia Inquirer*, May 1, 1921; Pennsylvania Academy scrapbooks, Archives of American Art, roll P56, frame 730. Even the most negative review of the show cited the intracity dialogue, claiming that a "group of New York cubists and futurists" had hoodwinked the Academy into "accepting what New York institutions have refused to open their doors to." See Alice Avon, "Academy Opens Its Doors to Cubists," *New York Telegraph*, April 16, 1921; Pennsylvania Academy scrapbooks, Archives of American Art, roll P56, frame 723.

88. See "Modern Art, " *Dial* 70 (January 1921): 112; (February 1921): 234–36; and *Dial* 71 (December 1921): 718–20. Louis Bouché, a writer and "Later Tendencies" exhibitor, concurred with McBride's assessment of the current Paris scene as "disappointing." See "Art Activities in Post-War Paris," *Arts* I (June–July 1921): 28–32. In fact, the January 1921 issue of the *Dial* remarked on how the "enthusiasm of French artists for Coney Island, ragtime, and other essentially American products continues scarcely less intense than their enthusiasm for African fetishes"; "Modern Art," *Dial*, 123–24.

89. See "Some Independents Invited To Exhibit Pictures," undated, unidentified clipping; William Yarrow clipping file, Library of the Pennsylvania Academy.

90. Untitled, undated, unidentified clipping fragment; William Yarrow clipping file, Library of the Pennsylvania Academy. For a chart of important modernist exhibitions, including Brooklyn's and the Metropolitan's, in these years, see Judith Zilczer, "Modern Art and Its Sources: Exhibitions in New York, 1910–1925," in Homer, *Avant-Garde Painting and Sculpture in America, 1910–25*, 166–70.

91. See untitled, undated, unidentified clipping; William Yarrow clipping file, Library of the Pennsylvania Academy, and "Comment on the Arts," *Arts* 1 (June–July 1921): 38.

92. See Joseph H. Appel, *The Business Biography of John Wanamaker, Founder and Builder* (New York: Macmillan, 1930), 128–31, 406.

93. Rodman Wanamaker's association with modernist currents ranged from the organization of annual photography exhibits at Belmaison to a promotion of French art deco. For a discussion of the progressive character of the Wanamaker Photographic Exhibitions, see W. G. Fitz, "A Few Thoughts on the Wanamaker Exhibition," *Camera* 22 (April 1918): 201–7. In 1906, Rodman Wanamaker sent Sayen and his wife, Jeannette Hope, a store designer, to Paris. Earlier, he had sponsored the European and Near Eastern studies of former Academy student Henry Ossawa Tanner. For general information on Rodman, see Appel, *John Wanamaker*, 120, 448–51. In 1919, Rodman Wanamaker's collection of "Paintings Done at the French Front" was featured at the Academy; see Archives of the Pennsylvania Academy.

94. "Academy To Have 3 Unusual Shows," *Philadelphia Inquirer*, March 20, 1921; Pennsylvania Academy scrapbooks, Archives of American Art, roll P56, frame 719.

95. See Francis J. Ziegler, "Modernism Invades Academy's Galleries," *Philadelphia Record*, April 9, 1921.

96. "Paxton's Paintings Take a $1000 Prize," *North American*, March 21, 1921; Pennsylvania Academy scrapbooks, Archives of American Art, roll P56, frame 720. In these years, Academy "moderns," like Carles and Breckenridge, as well as members of the Eight, more frequently appeared in the annuals than representatives of the New York avant-garde. See annual exhibition catalogues, Archives of the Pennsylvania Academy.

97. As Douglas has noted, the success in the twenties of new comic strips, like *Popeye* and *Krazy Kat*, among both the general public and the avant-garde (e.e. cummings considered George Herriman, *Krazy Kat*'s creator, the greatest "artist of the age"), influenced language as well as the visual arts. The comics' rude "linguistic explosions" often appeared in newspaper headlines about modernism, reflecting a popular "Who sez?" cultural retort regarding its aesthetic legitimacy; see *Terrible Honesty*, 54, 70, 451.

98. Ibid., 20.

99. See "Art That Looks Crazy on Display," *Philadelphia Public Ledger*, April 17, 1921; Pennsylvania Academy scrapbooks, Archives of American Art, roll P56, frame 722.

100. Apparently, others agreed, and Avon's polemic was liberally quoted in Philadelphia newspapers. See "'Green Cheese' Art Stirs N.Y. Critic," *Philadelphia Evening Bulletin*, April 19, 1921; Pennsylvania Academy scrapbooks, Archives of American Art, roll P56, frame 728.

101. See Avon, "Academy Opens Its Doors."

102. See "Art That Looks Crazy on Display." The then-current popularity of Sigmund Freud's theories of psychiatry, particularly in New York, may have accounted for some of this rhetoric; see Douglas, *Terrible Honesty*, 21.

103. See "Alienists Rap Cubist Art," *Philadelphia Evening Bulletin*, April 30, 1921; Pennsylvania Academy scrapbooks, Archives of American Art, roll P56, frame 730.

104. See "Comment on the Arts," *Arts* 1 (June–July 1921): 37; (August–September 1921): 44; Mary Fanton Roberts, "The Touchstone," *Arts* 1 (August–September 1921): 25–26; and assorted clippings; Pennsylvania Academy scrapbooks, Archives of American Art, roll P56, frames 730–45.

105. See "Expert Praises Modern Show," *Philadelphia Inquirer*.

106. Held from April 11 to May 9, Barnes's collection was part of a curious triple bill of special exhibitions, the other two being historical portraits by the Peale family and a group of paintings by Japanese artists; see Archives of the Pennsylvania Academy.

107. Initially, Barnes had wanted to display his collection of African sculpture along with the paintings—creating a so-called primitive context—but the Academy declined. See letter from Albert C. Barnes to John Frederick Lewis, March 21, 1923; Archives of the Pennsylvania Academy.

108. See Dorothy Grafly, "Old Portraits Praised, Modernist Art Decried," *North American*, April 15, 1923; Pennsylvania Academy scrapbooks, Archives of American Art, roll P57, frame 18.

109. For the twenties' critique of cultural philistinism and provincialism, see Dumenil, *Modern Temper*, 152–53. Also see Albert C. Barnes, "The Barnes Foundation," *New Republic* (March 14, 1923): 65–67.

110. For a discussion of the Academy's later attitude toward contemporary art, see Judith E. Stein, "Defining the Present in the Past: The Tradition of Contemporary Art at the Pennsylvania Academy of the Fine Arts," unpublished conference paper, 1989; Archives of the Pennsylvania Academy.

111. See letter from Alfred Stieglitz to John Andrew Myers, January 11, 1936; Annual Exhibition Correspondence, Archives of the Pennsylvania Academy.

112. See "Letters," *Arts* 1 (August–September 1921): 61.

"A WONDERFUL AGE" AND ITS "ARTISTIC ATOM-BOMBS":

EARLY AMERICAN MODERNISTS AND THEIR VIEWERS

Elizabeth Johns

This is a wonderful age we are living in now. Everyone has more creative liberty. The creative mind finds new ways and stops at no law laid down by, or piled upon us by lesser or non-creative minds. . . . It is great to live now! It is harder, but what of that? The hunger we have now! This new embrace of the universe. This great blending of various forms of expression.[1]

—Max Weber

Can we even imagine the excitement with which Max Weber and other modernist artists in the early years of the century were taking in one new idea after another? In conversation, in private reflection in their journals, and at their easels, artists entertained emerging theories about a fourth dimension in the universe, hypotheses about the human unconscious, hopes about the potential of the machine for social transformation, and questions about the meaning of human experience now that "civilization" was nestled in cities. They wrestled with the idea of a fourth dimension as the vast extension of the universe in all directions at once, beyond what their senses could perceive and their minds could grasp. Was not traditional representation of the observed world woefully inadequate?[2] And in the wake of the influential theories of Henri Bergson, that time was nonlinear and that reality was a flux rather than discrete moments, was not the restriction of an image to the "truth" of a single moment sadly outdated? Moreover, if images were to assimilate the formulations of Freud about the reality of dreams and memories and do justice to the dramatic changes skyscrapers were bringing to the cityscape, artists had daunting—but liberating—tasks before them.

Artists who met with open arms "this new embrace of the universe" tried to imagine how the variety of new ideas could be interwoven. Are we caught up unawares, they wondered, in a vast flow of energy? Given new possibilities of a vastly extended reality, what, then, is the meaning of nature? Would it be possible for new understandings about spatial realities to inform the uses to which we put machines? The way we conceive life in the cities? The very kind of images that we make?

Although these early modernists were a varied group—as different in artistic style as Marsden Hartley and Max Weber, in personality as John Marin and Walt Kuhn, and in theme as Charles Demuth and Georgia O'Keeffe—they shared three articles of faith in their imagemaking. These commonalities, rather than the stylistic isms in which they worked, provide the framework of this essay.

The first conviction they agreed on was that images captured interior experience. Such artists attempted to re-create in imagery the essential experience of being alert to the flow of an immense reality. They worked at being completely attentive to what Gertrude Stein called "the fullness and depth of each moment."[3] They were tuned to their experience of the senses, to the mystery of intellect and interiority, to the miracle of even the most ordinary thing. How could images convey one's astonishment at the world? How could artists shake off the age-old burden of received wisdom about this world, and how could imagemaking leave behind the exhausted formulations about what the world means and what we must do in it? How could artists, as Emerson put it, have an "original relation" with the universe?

The second faith that artists shared was that images alluded to an understanding of experience arrived at through social exchange. Artists got ideas by talking, listening, and looking at the work of others. In such salon settings as that of the Arensberg circle, Mabel Dodge, and Stieglitz's 291 gallery in New York, the Sketch Club in Philadelphia, and the Steins' home in Paris, groups of painters, writers, and patrons gathered to discuss books, pictures, and contemporary ideas.[4] One can imagine the effect of this process in the give-and-take of conversation. The personal mix consisted of some who were analytical, others who were emotional, some who were eager to invoke the long historical perspective, and others alive to every implication of the immediate present. Some were philosophical, others full of statistics. Some were dictatorial. Each group had its antiauthoritarians given to making outrageous statements to repudiate the past; each group also had members who were gentler in their probing, unwilling to throw out the past completely. Artists were both listeners *and* talkers, nonartists were talkers and encouragers. Max Weber testified to the character of this kind of experience in describing the Steins' salons:

This salon was a sort of international clearing house of ideas and matters of art, for the young and aspiring artists from all over the world. Lengthy and involved discussions took place, with Leo Stein as moderator and participator. Here one felt free to throw artistic atom-bombs, and many cerebral explosions did take place.[5]

Artists took the give-and-take of conversation to their easels, producing a flow of experimental work. They asked: Is this what we face in the new century? Or, rather, do these forms tellingly evoke it? What are the traditions of the past that we can adopt? What can we allude to and reorient in order to make clear the differences between the past and the present?

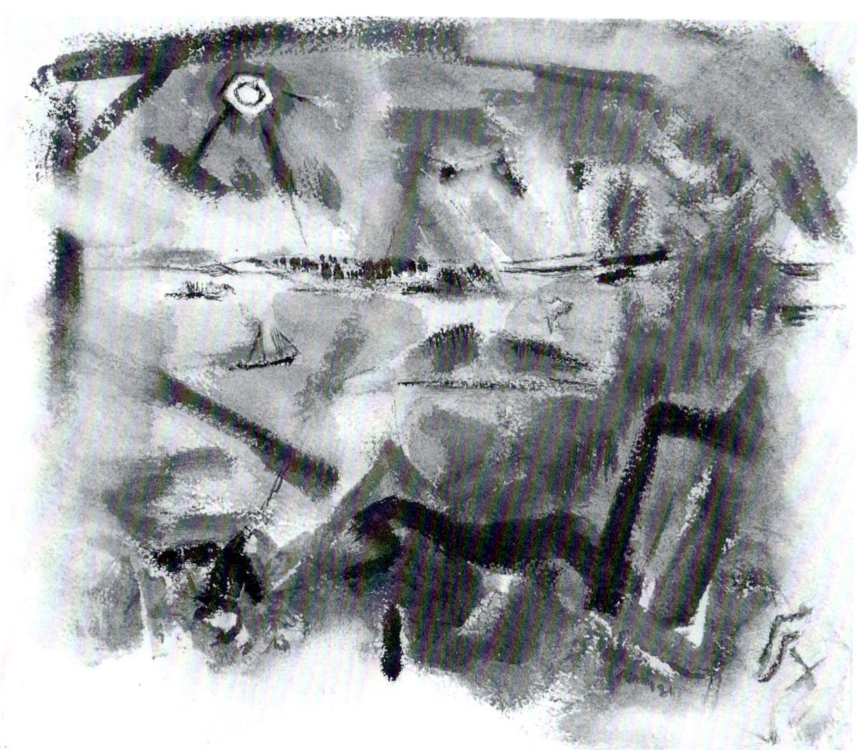

1. John Marin
Sun, Sea, Land—Maine
1921
Watercolor over charcoal on heavy off-white wove paper
16½ x 19⁷⁄₁₆"
Museum of American Art of the Pennsylvania Academy of the Fine Arts. John S. Phillips Bequest, 1876 (By exchange: acquired from the Samuel S. White, III, and Vera White Collection, given to the Philadelphia Museum of Art in 1967), 1985.21

And third, these modernists saw images as experiments rather than finished products. Being modern meant setting aside the old assumptions about representation, assumptions that had arisen from and thereby evoked an older, now unsatisfying way of defining the universe and humanity's place in it. Because no one could say with confidence what the universe must now mean, imagemaking that attempted to evoke this unknown put forth possibilities rather than certainties. As artists saw, in intense self-consciousness, their task was not even understood, their directions not yet clearly defined. The earlier way of looking at images was that they *resolved* uncertainty; in this period, they *posited* uncertainty.

The works shown at the Pennsylvania Academy of the Fine Arts in the "Exhibition of Paintings and Drawings Showing the Later Tendencies in Art," in 1921—many of them on view in the present exhibition—expressed these various dimensions of engagement with the new world coming into being.

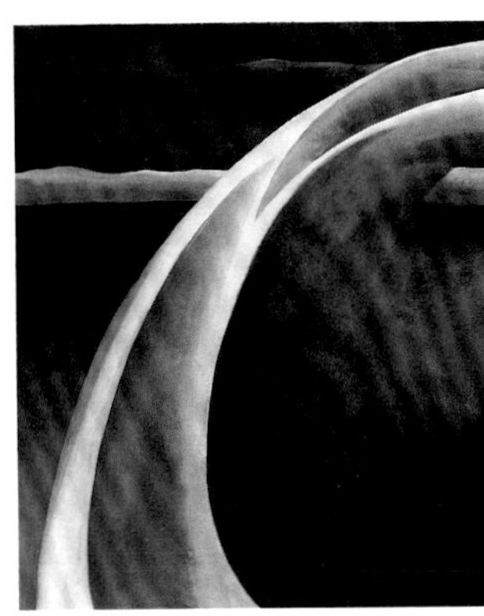

2. Georgia O'Keeffe
Orange and Red Streak
1919
Oil on canvas
27 x 23"
Philadelphia Museum of Art, Bequest of Georgia O'Keeffe for the Alfred Stieglitz Collection

Just as there were many ideas afloat, so there were many inspirations for images.

One inspiration underlay works by such artists as John Marin, Marsden Hartley, and Georgia O'Keeffe. These painters, all of whom knew each other in several social settings, experienced a heightened receptivity to nature on both sensual and spiritual levels. Living the role of the artist as mystic—in consummate attentiveness to sensory experience—they urged that if viewers, too, could only listen and see, they would know themselves in the presence of astonishing natural processes. Pictures could evoke that awe. Marsden Hartley spoke for an entire generation when he wrote, "The inherent magic in the appearance of the world about me, engrossed and amazed me. No cloud or blossom or bird or human ever escaped me, I think."[6]

Hartley's images reveal that he derived his very emotional being from nature. He had begun his career in Maine as a landscapist; after a brief foray into other subjects in the midteens, he returned to this first love—land, radiant with nature's indwelling spirit. Among the substantial number of artists and writers who went to New Mexico for inspiration of a very different topography, Hartley absorbed the strangeness of the landscape into aesthetic memories that endured for a lifetime. In his *New Mexico Landscape* (1919) [p. 44], he presents an earthy nature animated by a visible spirit. His heavy colors present mountains, hills, mesas, trees, and clouds that undulate with the moving spirit of nature. The houses seem to be only temporary presences in these sacred spaces.

John Marin, too, confronted nature in amazement. A New Jersey native who had always enjoyed the outdoors, he "discovered" Maine in 1914—along with a number of other artists who drank up the coastline's rugged beauty. His *Sun, Sea, Land—Maine* (1921) [fig. 1] presents hints of nature that convey its majestic otherness. Hovering over the upper left on the canvas is a charcoal trapezoid (within which is a circle) radiating blue. On the right horizon are brilliant splashes of red, yellow, and orange, presaging the sun about to rise in the east. A boat floats in the large, central blue lake, and passages of green invoke the Maine forest. Across the right foreground, a heavy and angled charcoal line suggests the presence of the viewer, pushing us back so that we envision the landscape as available to us but distinctly separate. Here, as in other images, Marin worked on a small scale; for him, size did not indicate the grandeur of nature but nature's intensity, especially fragmentary intensity. His creed became, "The fewer strokes I can take, the better the picture."[7]

Before Georgia O'Keeffe even knew both Marin and Hartley, whose work she would come to admire, she first conceived of painting in the presence of nature. Working in the open spaces of western Texas, her early abstractions searingly express the experience of light coming over the horizon. In her *Orange and Red Streak* (1919) [fig. 2], for instance, with powerful color and dynamic movement, one senses the grand continuum of the universe—of time, the heavenly bodies, the vast dimensions of space, the mystery of color and light, and the human observer present in only the briefest of moments. Many found her work closest to the elusive, expressive power of music. Not a person who talked easily about art, O'Keeffe assessed her early work in color: "I found that I could say things with color and shapes that I couldn't say in any other way—things that I had no words for."[8] In the landscapes of O'Keeffe, as well as of Marin and Hartley, we are in the presence of an original consciousness wrestling with the universe, of a sensibility that notices and connects every detail to a transcendent power.

Some of the modernists who were enthralled with nature got swept up in a widespread excitement about the potential of the city. John Marin's *From the Window of "291," Looking Down Fifth Avenue* (1911) is alive with movement, even cacophony. It pulses with the optimism about the city, of which Marin wrote, in 1911:

I have just started some downtown stuff, and to pile these great houses one upon another with paint as they do pile themselves up there so beautiful, so fantastic—at times one is afraid to look at them but feels like running away. The whole city is alive; buildings, people, all are alive; and the more they move me the more I feel them to be alive. It is this "moving of me" that I try to express, so that I may recall the spell I have been under and behold the expression of the different emotions that have been called into being. How am I to express what I feel so that its expression will bring me back under the spells? Shall I copy facts photographically? I see great forces at work; great movements; the large buildings and the small buildings; the warring of the great and the small; influences of one mass on another greater or smaller mass. Feelings are aroused which give me the desire to express the reaction of these "pull forces," those influences which play with one another; great masses pulling smaller masses, each subject in some degree to the other's power.[9]

Like Marin in the heart of New York, the immigrant Joseph Stella was taken with the spectacle of urban entertainment. This subject was only superficially distinct from the throbbing hills and clouds in a Western landscape, for it, too, reflected the artist's faith in a sensory continuum; this one, however, contained people, buildings, lights, smells, and sounds. Wide-eyed at the abundance in America, in contrast with the poverty in his native Italy, Stella described the electrifying effect on his art of his first vision of Coney Island, for many, at the time, a quintessential symbol of American energy:

I had been working along the lines of the old masters, seeking to portray a civilization long since dead. And then one night I went on a bus ride to Coney Island during Mardi Gras. That incident was what started me on the road to success. Arriving at the Island I was instantly struck by the dazzling array of lights. It seemed as if they were in conflict. I was struck with the thought that here was what I had been unconsciously seeking for many years.[10]

Stella's *Battle of Lights, Coney Island, Mardi Gras* (1913) [p. 59] is filled with hints of extravagant rides, confetti, noise, lights flashing for entertainment and food, sideshows, fragments of signage and advertisements, and boisterous crowds. Exhibited in 1914 at the Montross Gallery, along with one hundred other American modernist works, the painting raised eyebrows about modernism just as it and other works were to do in Philadelphia in 1921.

Marin, O'Keeffe, and Stella celebrated each moment as bursting with the unexpected. Other members of the same social circles took a different tack; they expressed the unseen forces of reality as leading to a reassuring order. The locus of this order, they felt, was the social environment—scenes human beings had created and in which they lived. In attempting to be faithful to the experience of the moment, they re-created the perception of color and shape, followed by its interpretation. Some, like Morton L. Schamberg, saw city experiences through the perception of color. A frequenter of the Arensberg circle, in his small *View from the Side Boxes (Opera)* (ca. 1910–11) [fig. 3], he presents a scene at a concert hall, perhaps Philadelphia's Academy of Music. The brilliant pastel and oil image, with blues over purple, green over orange, hard yellow, and separating lines in darker violets and blacks, creates a space that is alive with color. Even when Schamberg turned to landscapes, as in *Landscape, Bridge* (1915) [fig. 4], he created them with color. Dazzled by what his friend Marcel Duchamp called "the beauty which the makers of machines lent to their work," he began painting machine forms that seem to have symbolized, for him, the ordering process that emerged from the great flux.[11] Color, however, modified the potential coldness of mechanical forms. In his *Painting IV (Mechanical Abstraction)* (1916) [fig. 5], each of the surfaces of this unidentifiable machine is modulated in color and tone. The form seems alive. Indeed, a touch of red gives the effect of a tongue on the mouth of the machine. Here, as in the landscapes of other modernists, the image suggests an environment that is itself changing and in process.

In conveying his own primary relationship with the universe, H. Lyman Saÿen also used color and order as signs of a new understanding of reality. His *Abstract Landscape* (1915–16) [p. 55] organizes park forms through bright colors (sailboats, gardens, ponds, walks) and, in an orderly progression, pushes them back into the distance. Adjacent colors, such as orange and green and red and blue, contend with each other to create space. The eye works to stabilize the image, which, viewed section by section, is flat, but, as a whole, proposes a lively depth. One of the most intellectual of the modernists—and active in the discussion circles in Philadelphia and New York—Saÿen carefully formulated theories of what he was doing:

Modern art . . . is all spontaneity and requires an equally spontaneous apprehension. To feel it requires a quickening of the spirit. . . . Popular sense has supposed the new type of art as representing peculiar emotions. It is more than that, it is the emotions

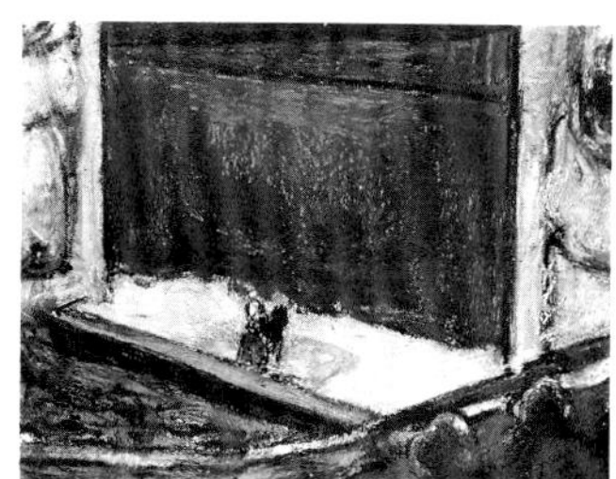

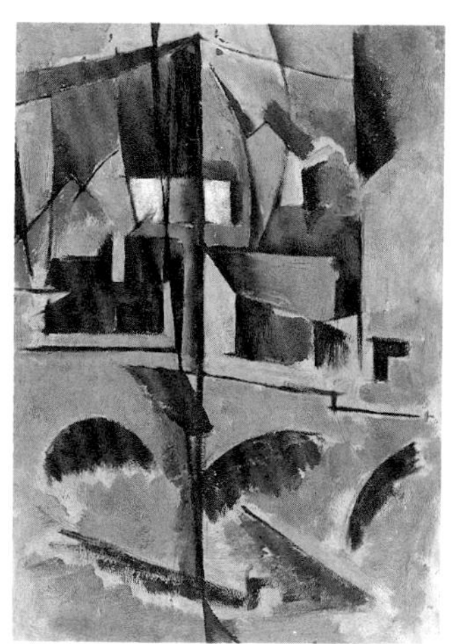

3. Morton L. Schamberg
View from the Side Boxes (Opera)
Ca. 1910–11
Pastel on board
5½ x 7¼"
Museum of American Art of the Pennsylvania Academy of the Fine Arts. Purchased with funds from the Joseph E. Temple Fund, Mrs. Robert P. Levy, Mrs. Kenneth W. Gemmill, and Frank and Betsy Goodyear, 1982.4

4. Morton L. Schamberg
Landscape, Bridge
1915
Oil on panel
13⅝ x 9⅝"
Philadelphia Museum of Art, Gift of Dr. and Mrs. Ira Leo Schamberg

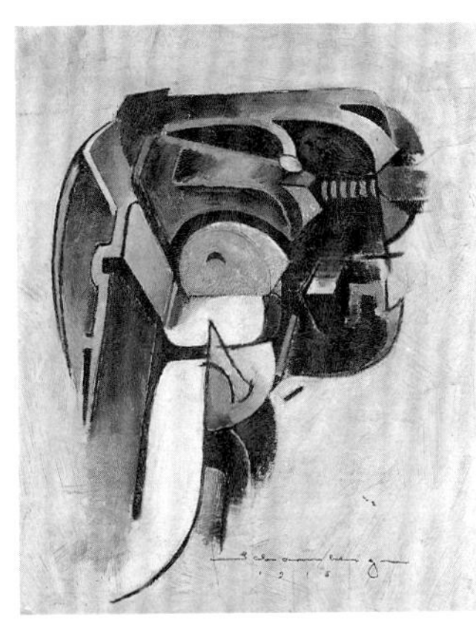

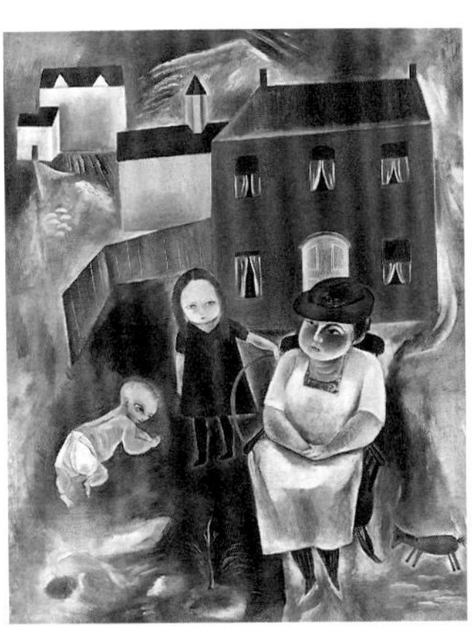

5. Morton L. Schamberg
Painting IV (Mechanical Abstraction)
1916
Oil on panel
13¾ x 10¾″
Philadelphia Museum of Art, The Louise and Walter Arensberg Collection

6. Yasuo Kuniyoshi
Maine Family
Ca. 1922–23
Oil on canvas
30 x 24″
The Phillips Collection, Washington, D.C.

themselves. In fact emotion is no longer the name for the act, neither of its creation nor its apprehension. Perception touches nearer the mark.

Saÿen, too, felt the connection of image with a transcendent reality. "[Painting's] rhythm is that of the pulse, its beauty the law of God."[12]

For Weber, the artist who embraced the universe with such joy, matter throbbed with spiritual reality. In and out of various conversational circles, Weber wrote in his *Essays on Art*, of 1916:

Things, objects, mutely cry to us, "Touch us, taste us, feel us, see us, understand us, learn us, make us more than we are through your association, through your tactile and spiritual intimacy.". . . An artist should hope to evoke with grains of matter the very atoms of color and time. He should feel as though he empowered the silent with speech and the static with motion; and should seem to angle the light and to impregnate the three dimensions with a spiritual fourth dimension. If not spiritually conceived or transfigured by great inspiration, matter is dead.[13]

And yet, in his assessment of New York, Max Weber was no idealist. In his *Rush Hour, New York* (1915) [p.61], the pale and relentlessly successive geometric forms and fragments suggest precision, mechanization, and repetition—all threats posed by industrialization. In the world of this image, in the discrepancies between the individuals in the streets and the towering impersonality of skyscrapers, human activity is subordinate. Weber seems to throw Marin's earlier optimism open to question: What is the future? What is the meaning of the changes under way?

Other artists in these circles also evoked puzzlement about the new worlds in the making. Yasuo Kuniyoshi, rather than painting the beauty of a Maine landscape, set forth the inexplicable social worlds of the rural population in images that we now identify as surrealistic. His *Maine Family* (ca. 1921) [fig.6] is a bizarre evocation of a mother and father (almost completely hidden behind the mother in a most peculiar way) and two children—a girl whose face is beyond her years and a small baby who is crawling on the ground. A toy, or a small family pet, stands on the right. All the figures are deliberately rendered primitive. In the crowded background are houses with a preternatural presence, the heavy red of the nearest one and the draped Victorian windows spaced regularly across its facade deepening the ominous quality of the picture. Marin had floated free from human associations that were unsettling; Kuniyoshi fastened onto them as unforgettable.

If Kuniyoshi is a puzzle, John Covert's work is a thorough mystery. Of all the artists and talkers in the Arensberg circle, Covert was among the most intellectual. Fascinated by mathematics and new scientific theories, he was quiet and reticent, taking everything in until a sudden "conversion" in 1915 to the possibilities of modernist imagemaking. Of his long gestation, he told Rudi Blesh, in 1956, that when he was in Paris, "I didn't get to know a modern artist, or see a modern show, or even meet the Steins. It's incredible. I must have lived in armor."[14] One of his most arcane works, *The Temptation of Saint Anthony* (1916) [p.38] evokes a traditional religious subject as though to debunk the world behind it. Barely perceived female forms are subordinate to geometric surfaces; in one respect, the picture is a meditation on sexuality.

Just as any group of talkers contains members who explode in emotion, members who chime in with brilliant analytic remarks, and still others who stop conversation cold with witty irony, so the modernist painters—all of them participants in salons and coteries whose memberships overlapped—represented many different responses to the possibilities of modern picturemaking. The response that most represents the later phase of the American modernist experiments—after about 1916—is irony. Introduced in force in conversational circles by the dadaists, this tone of doubt might well have flourished anyway. For irony, which holds disparate views in balance, draws its lifeblood from a social world, partaking of conversation with a group who understands and outsiders who do not. It can project amusement or, in its sharper moments, bitterness. The amusement is not so much at the human tendency to be arrogant (and wrong) but at our human predicament; we are experiencing a major change in our philosophical and scientific underpinnings and see the smallness with which we speak. Irony withholds conclusion.

The consummate ironist was Charles Demuth [fig.7], an intimate of Stieglitz, a familiar in the

Steins' salons in Paris, and a member of the Arensberg circle. Full of reservations about virtually everything, Demuth was a master of understatement. He described the relationship of his work to the highly emotional images of Marin: "John Marin and I drew our inspiration from the same sources. He brought his up in buckets and spilled much along the way. I dipped mine out with a teaspoon but I never spilled a drop."[15] Demuth cast his skeptical eye on the putative promise of industrialization and its relationship to the human spirit. His *Aucassin and Nicolette* (1921) [p. 40], for example, the work that, inevitably, evoked alarmed commentary when exhibited, depicts factories above which a phallic smokestack rises side by side with a cylindrical water tower. He named the work after a medieval tale of frustrated sexual love, thereby wittily linking the shapes of mechanical objects to sexuality and, by extension, implying the potential of mechanization to toll the death knell for human warmth. His light colors further distance the depicted buildings from concrete reality, as do the veils in the atmosphere created by his lines of force. In *From the Garden of the Château* (1921) (château was his name for his Lancaster home), he again used a title to hold in disjunction the relationship between present and past. The view for American city dwellers of a proliferation of factories is a dramatic contrast to that of an older European class who looked out on gardens. His irony is multiple; it calls into question the proliferation of factories, and it places an unexamined faith about progress against a backdrop of an older world in which natural beauty and sexuality were the major subjects for artists. Demuth proposes, but ducks, concluding: Have we truly progressed? What have we lost? Where are we going? His works were both serious meditations and in-jokes, and that arrogance, as well as its underlying irreverence for the pieties about modern life, was part of the social code of the talkers and writers and artists who probed the new world.

Demuth used irony to undercut the industrial landscape, relying on titles to provide the social connections and to stimulate laughter as well as reflection. Florine Stettheimer, on the other hand, depicted the human beings who were doing the talking and the laughing, the proclaiming and the objecting. Among her closest friends was Marcel Duchamp; she also moved in the social circles of

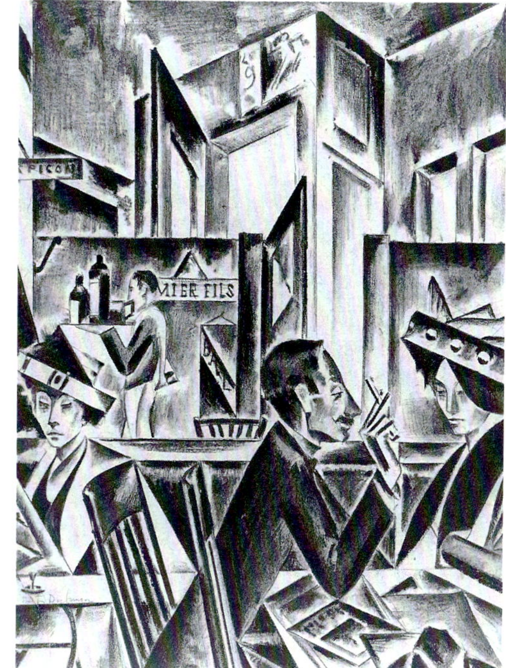

Katherine Dreier and was a friend of the critic Henry McBride. Her very techniques demanded a viewership in the know. Calling her paintings "sentimental histories" of her associates and family, in some the same character appears several times. Not only does this technique allude to a medieval tradition of "continuous narrative," in which an image within one frame traces a sequence of actions, but it visualizes the new sense of the complexity of time, the simultaneity of events in memory. It celebrates the several dimensions of personality and captures, as Carl Van Vechten was to write, the gaiety and "riotous" spirit of jazz music. In both *Asbury Park South* (1920) [p. 60] and *Picnic at Bedford Hills* (1919) [fig. 8], characters float through several stages of their own experience. *Picnic at Bedford Hills* presents, in almost abrasive color, five languid figures enjoying the quiet conversation, private absorption, and preoccupation with an elegant menu associated with an upper-class leisurely afternoon. In contrast, *Asbury Park South* presents a scene at a beach frequented by black people, in which Stettheimer condenses weightless figures (some of them recognizable as her friends) to poses, gestures, and costumes that peg the personality. Many are arrested in the motions of dancing, and the vibrant colors pulse with the goings-on of a lively and self-consciously elegant beach crowd. In these works, as in her unusual portraits, Stett-

7. Preston Dickinson
Café Scene (Portrait of Charles Demuth)
Ca. 1912–14
Charcoal and black chalk on tan wove paper
18 x 13¾"
Collection of Mr. and Mrs. Meyer P. Potamkin

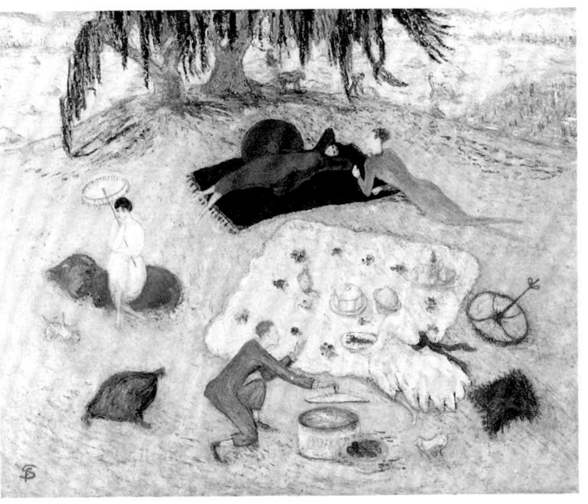

8. Florine Stettheimer
Picnic at Bedford Hills
1919
Oil on canvas
40$\frac{5}{16}$ x 50¼″
Museum of American Art of the Pennsylvania Academy of the Fine Arts. Gift of Ettie Stettheimer, 1950.2

heimer's irony was turned on the group itself—on the social world of modernism. She saw through its pretensions and its pronouncements, and she participated in the whole process with delight.

Perhaps no image so successfully points up the tensions and absurdities of high-minded talk as Marius de Zayas's caricature of John Marin and Alfred Stieglitz [fig. 9]. Here, Stieglitz, as the self-appointed expert in modernism who called for freshness and new visions, leads the way for Marin, one of the artists he sponsored in his gallery. He is implacable in his arrogance, with an authoritative stare behind the spectacles that hide him, and funny in his bulk, looking out at the viewer with a trapezoidal face that is unreadable. We see Marin from the side; he, like many others, is marching along to the modern tune. Yet, he keeps his distance, his waist making an indented angle that responds to the jutting angle of Stieglitz's elbow. Marin's bushy hair prevents us from seeing his eyes at all. His nose just touches the point of Stieglitz's shoulder; he follows Stieglitz, he's on his trail, he's even nosy, but he, too, with closed mouth and receding chin blocking interference, keeps his cards close to his chest. Both men are stubbornly themselves.

These are some of the pictures that a new generation of imagemakers created in an attempt to visualize a changed—and changing—world. They were citizens of a world that placed new emphasis on experience, social bonding, and experimentation. And this is precisely what upset viewers and critics. Was observable reality no longer meaningful? If pictures were to translate experience, and experience were interior—that is, subjective rather than exterior or objective—how would viewers be able to validate an artist's vision? Since no tradition had been constructed yet of translating reverence for nature into color detached from the depiction of nature, of pondering material forces at work by making rapid brushstrokes and interrupting the field of representation, of conveying intellectual openness through disjunctive spaces and incomplete forms, how could viewers claim a commonality of experience with artists? How could they judge the success of what was before them? Were artists yet another professionalizing group that was fragmenting the citizenry and taking its own competence into a closed universe, leaving out the ordinary citizen? And in a country devoted to democracy, as distinct from European privilege, was not the very meaning of American national identity threatened by this artistic impudence? How could art take as its subject matter what was utilitarian and of recent vintage rather than beautiful and eternally true? Even more fundamental, how could art be merely experimental? Were not artists responsible for conclusions rather than hypotheses? For consolation rather than doubt? The proposition that images could be as much a part of figuring out the new world as technology and the scientific laboratory gave an almost unbearable challenge to looking at recent art.

Such doubts, and they were genuine and profound, led to complaints at the Pennsylvania Academy's "Later Tendencies" exhibition, of 1921, that representation had been abandoned and nothing sensible put in its place. Some complained that "clashing colors" and "crazy compositions" had replaced good design.[16] "Brightness is the thing, with such minor virtues as composition, meaning and treatment entirely secondary," wrote another reviewer, bemoaning the lack of craftsmanship with attacks on "the frenzied attempts at originality of a John Marin" and "Stella's skyrocketing *Coney Island*, fatally facile yet not intelligent."[17]

Many expressed great distress that the figures on the canvases were in pieces. Even when traditional subjects had been undertaken, such as Walt Kuhn's woman in *The City* (1919) [p. 45], critics objected to his "recloth[ing of an] extinct tradition" to make a picture of "an overfed vulgar brewer's daughter, who has evidently come in contact with poison ivy and is all swelled up over it."[18] The artist-critic Francis Ziegler, who found the idea of art as experimental art "innocent," drew the line at distortion of the human figure:

[O]ther forms of modernism [are] not so innocuous. The reference here is to the distortions of the naked human body . . . to produce gross caricatures of the human figure, is to commit a sin against the temple of the Holy Ghost, and an outrage against decency.[19]

Viewers and critics rallied for comfort in front of Thomas Hart Benton's solidly modeled *The Beach* (1920) [p. 36] and Arthur B. Davies's asexual, tapestrylike *Maenad Arabesques*. In fact, the *Inquirer* critic, Bushnell Dimond, praised Davies's picture as "perhaps the finest individual achievement of the whole show."[20]

Critics disliked intensely the suspicion that the new art would leave them out. In their reviews, they brandished the terms "initiated" and "uninitiated" as synonyms for artists and the public. New York critic Alice Avon crusaded for truth: "Through a loud blowing of trumpets the [Pennsylvania] Academy of [the] Fine Arts has been hoodwinked by a group of New York cubists and futurists."[21] Some even associated the wilder experiments with a cult. They insisted that art could not be made by a committee. Avon assured her readers that "*groups*" don't create "great works of art"; rather, "the masterpieces and the truly big works today . . . are being conceived and executed by individuals and individuals only." Academies, she lectured, train individual genius in the great tradition: "They are an essential product of and for civilization." What the Academy's "Later Tendencies" exhibition put forward, she concluded, was the informal, incomplete work of artists who had turned their backs on the academic tradition and, thus, on civilization.[22]

More than a few viewers complained about the disdain for seriousness radiated by the pictures. Dimond wrote that Weber's *Chinese Restaurant* (1915) was painted "to reassure the frightened futurist suspicious of excessive intelligibility." And he berated Demuth:

Demuth['s] cleverness has snatched the whip from his hand and ridden him like a legendary demon. When he will, he paints well, with a "brainy" quality best exemplified in his Business *(1921) [fig. 10]. When freakishness seizes him, he can perpetrate such dry jokes as the* Aucassin and Nicolette, *which (unless the catalogue lies) consists of two buildings.*[23]

Several critics threw the disdain back at the artists:

It takes a tremendous amount of imagination to paint ultra-modern pictures. The extremists themselves admit it, and the public is ready to believe it. Furthermore, it requires a tremendous amount of imagination to discover in some of the pictures the real significance as purposed by the artists. More, alas! than many of us possess. . . . "But," to quote an official of the Academy board, "the men and women whose work is now on exhibition here take themselves and their work very seriously. There may be more in it than we can see. Who knows?"[24]

Those who were inclined to be cautious in their condemnation picked up on the title of the exhibition as conveying only "tendencies" rather than definitive styles. Ziegler emphasized the implications of the term. Claiming that the exhibition was actually a kind of retrospective, he noted: "It must be admitted that [the artists] have succeeded in putting together a comprehensive collection of canvases which represents many phases of the modernistic movement."[25] Dimond congratulated the organizers on creating an exhibition that was not narrow-minded but, rather, "even a catholic inclination toward fashions. . . . In the main, the exhibition is only advanced in the sense that it would have shocked Sully, the Pre-Raphaelites, or the later Dutch masters."[26] Ziegler reassured an angry readership: "What will come of all these influences it is hard to tell."[27]

The ironist Marius de Zayas understood viewers' reservations and had superb advice for those who would reexamine their premises. In *A Study of the Modern Evolution of Plastic Expression*, he urged viewers to lay aside their conceptions about what art should be. Placing art in the realm of the temporal as opposed to the timeless, he discredited the traditional association of creativity with the artist. "Nothing is done by man which has not its fundamental basis outside of man," de Zayas wrote. Within the human sphere, times change; what human beings decide is art and make as art changes through the ages. The best artist, he argued, is sensitive to the spirit of the times. "The artist being part of the community reflects the soul of the community in which he lives; not of the community in the sense of the general masses, but in the sense of those elements through which he comes in

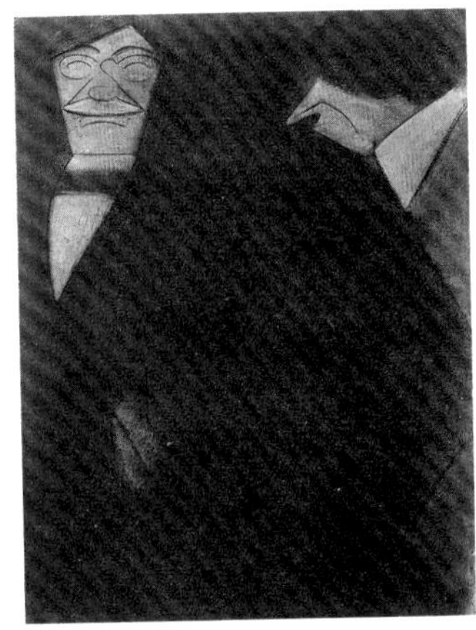

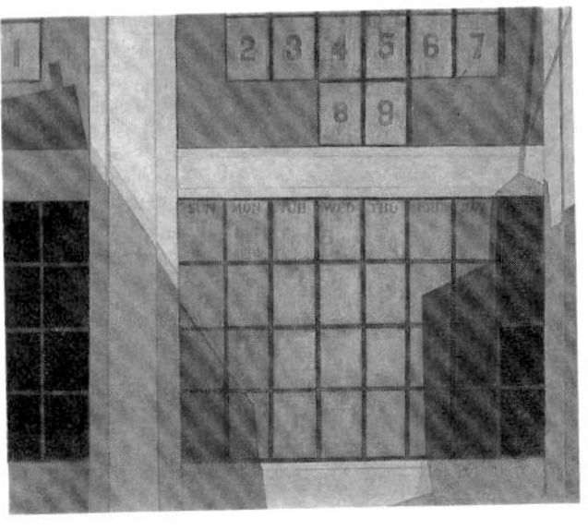

9. Marius de Zayas
John Marin and Alfred Stieglitz
Ca. 1912
Charcoal on paper
24¼ x 18⅝"
Lent by The Metropolitan Museum of Art, Alfred Stieglitz Collection, 1949

10. Charles Demuth
Business
1921
Oil on canvas
20 x 24¼"
The Art Institute of Chicago, Alfred Stieglitz Collection, 1949.529.

38

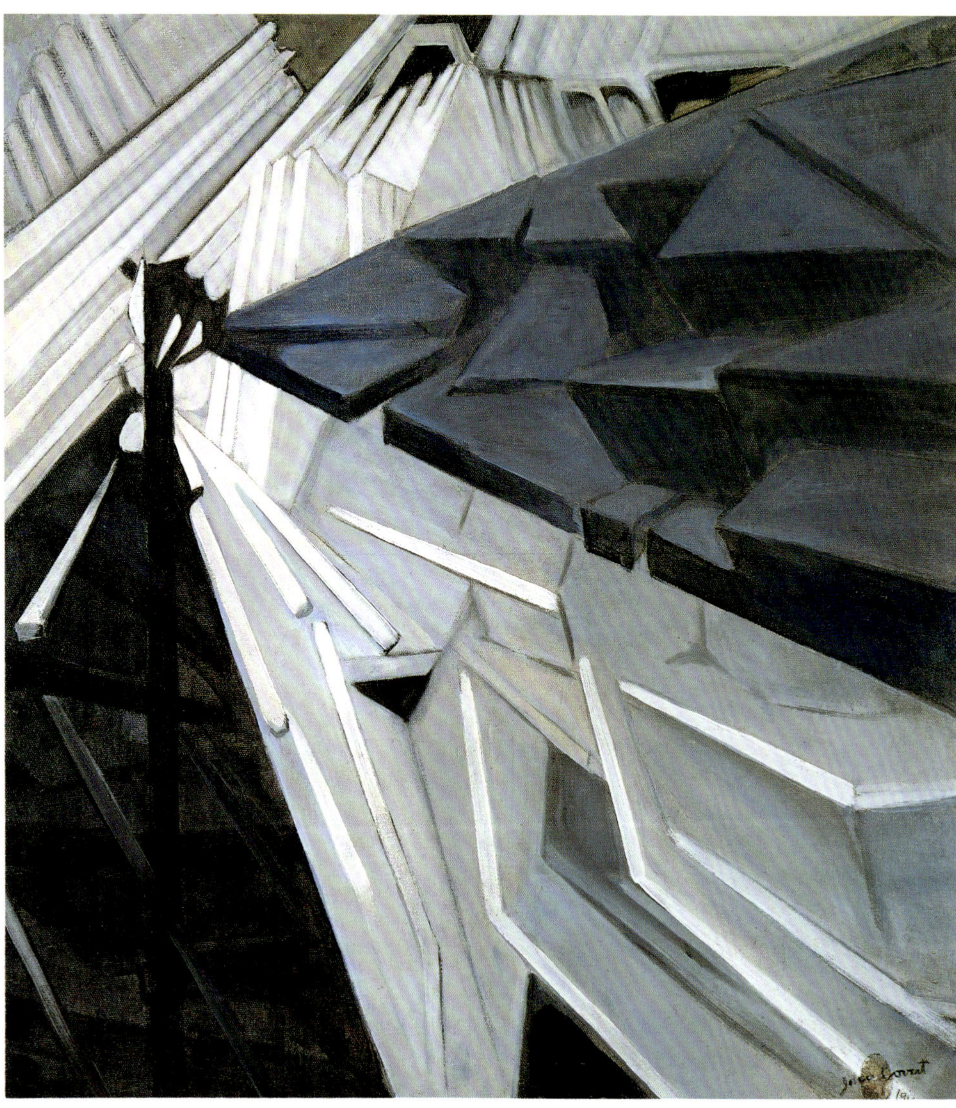

John Covert

• *Temptation of Saint Anthony*, 1916, oil on canvas, 25 11/16 x 23 3/4"
Yale University Art Gallery, Gift of Collection Société Anonyme

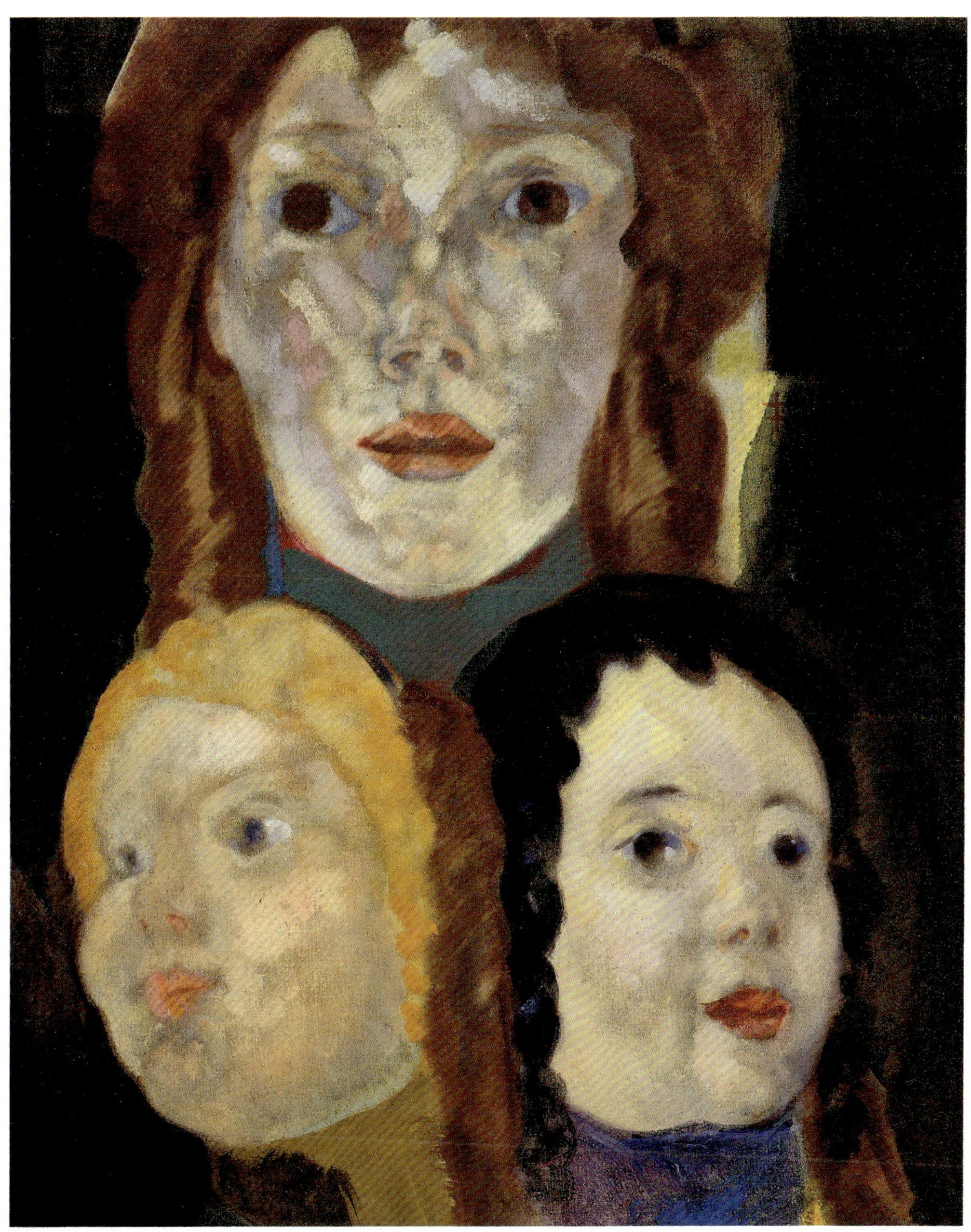

Arthur B. Davies

* *Three Masks*, ca. 1920, oil on canvas, 28 x 23"

Collection Denver Art Museum. Museum purchase

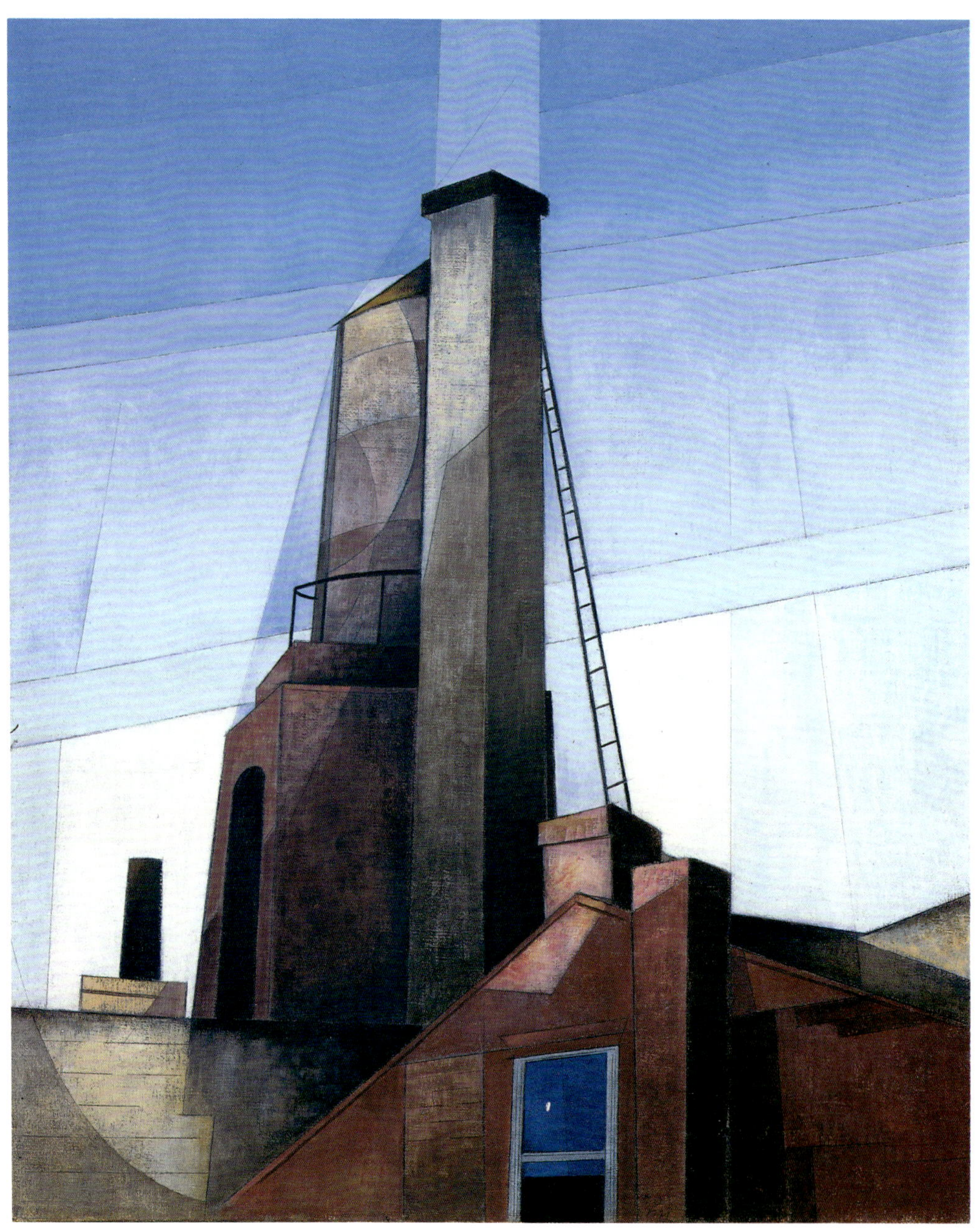

Charles Demuth

* *Aucassin and Nicolette*, 1921, oil on canvas, 24 ⅛ x 20″

Columbus Museum of Art, Ohio: Gift of Ferdinand Howald

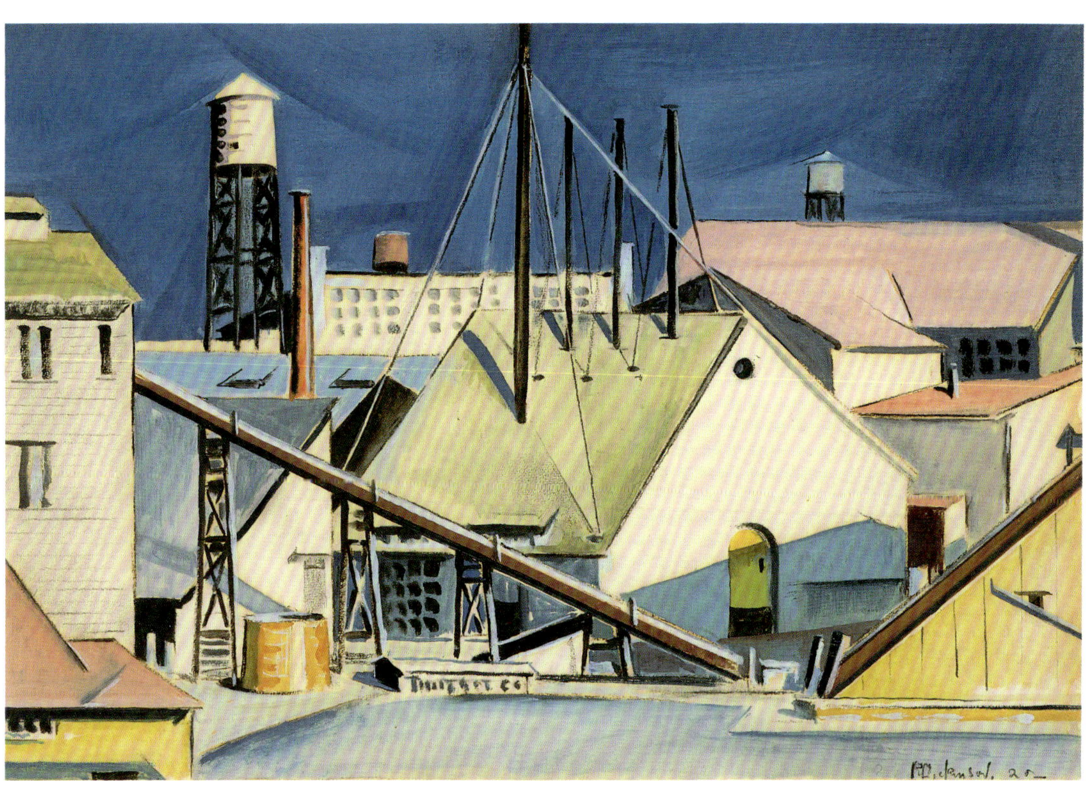

Preston Dickinson

* *Factories*, 1920, pencil and gouache on paper, 14 x 20 ¼"
Collection of The Newark Museum, Gift of Ruth, Rachel, and
Toby Armour in memory of their father, Bernard R. Armour, 1955

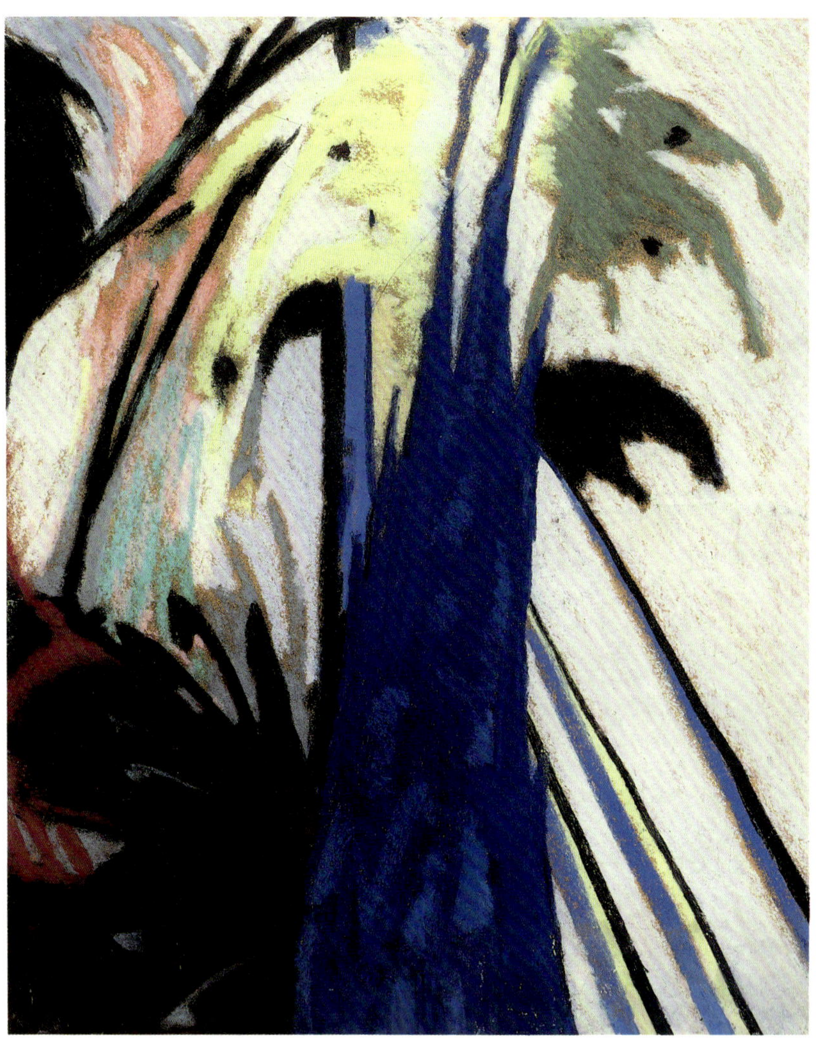

Arthur G. Dove

* *League of Nations*, ca. 1914, pastel on thin paper, mounted on pulp board, 21 5/16 x 17 13/16"
Georgia Museum of Art, University of Georgia; Eva Underhill Holbrook Memorial Collection of American Art, gift of Alfred Heber Holbrook. GMOA 45.32

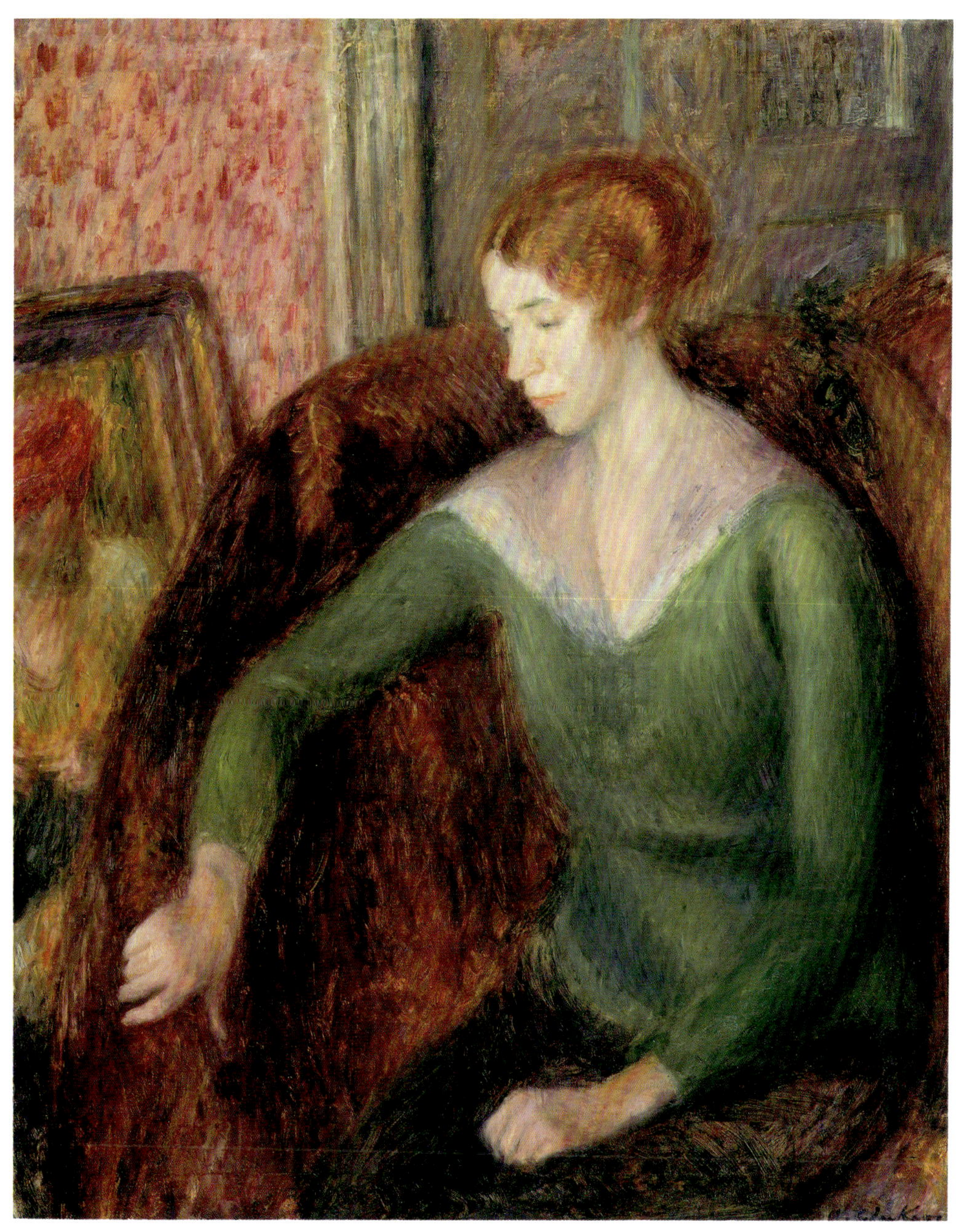

William Glackens

* *Finnish Woman*, 1920, oil on canvas, 32 x 26″

Courtesy of Kraushaar Galleries, New York

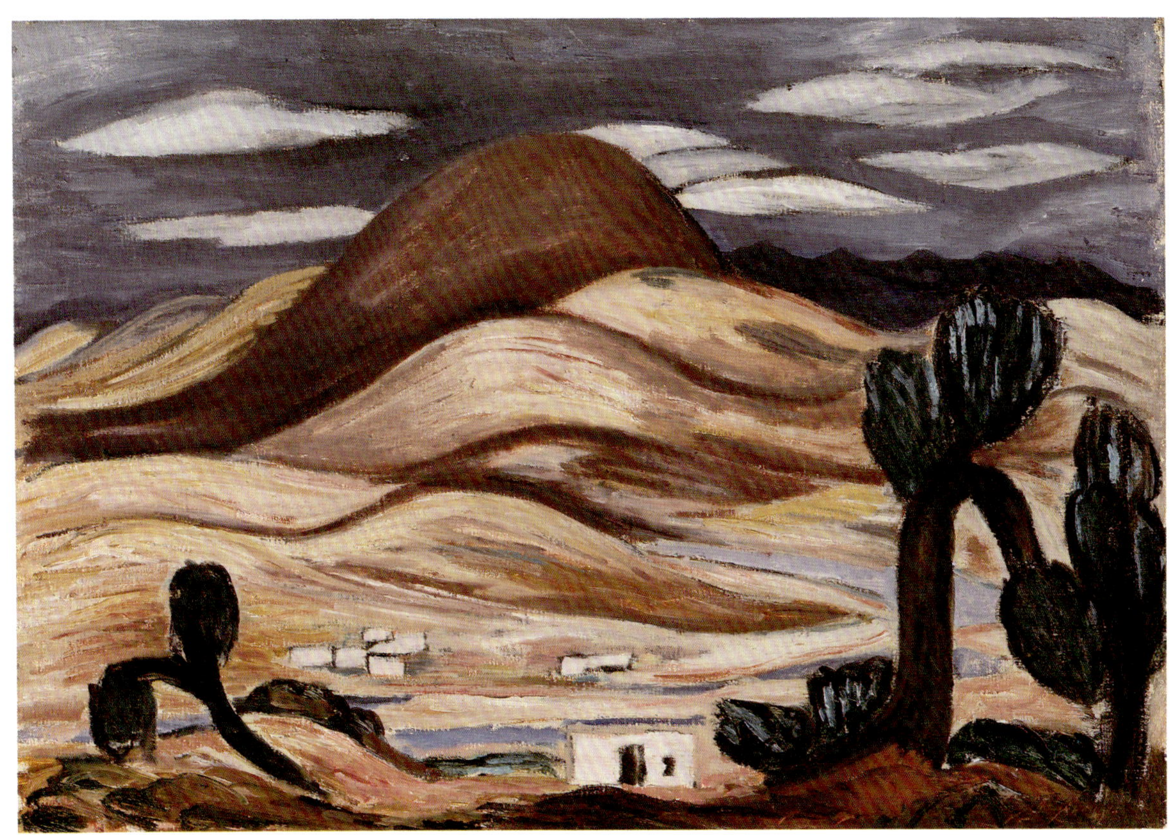

Marsden Hartley

New Mexico Landscape, 1919, oil on canvas, 17⅞ x 26″

Philadelphia Museum of Art, The Alfred Stieglitz Collection

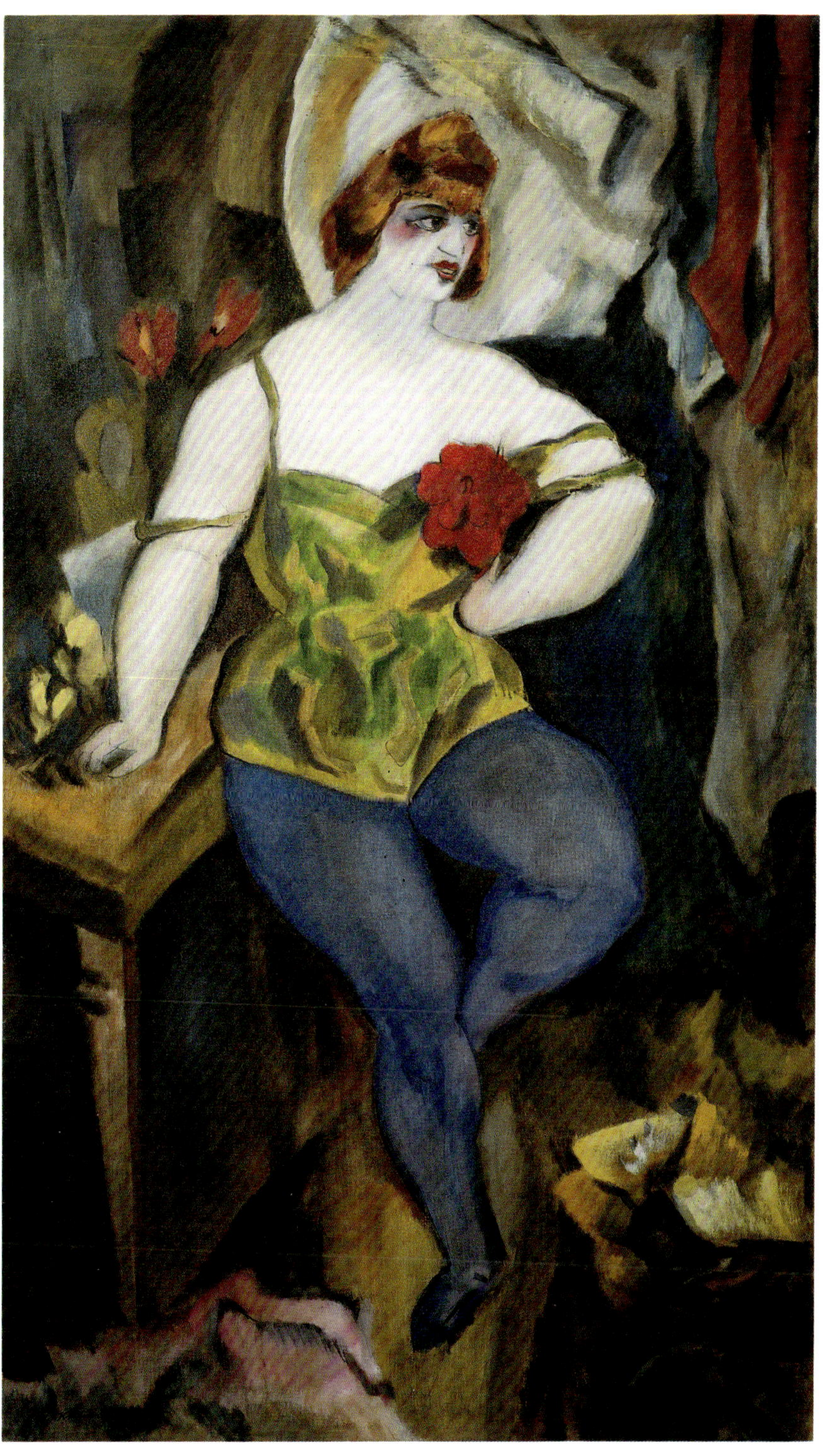

Walt Kuhn

* *The City*, 1919, oil on canvas, 89 x 52″

Courtesy of Kennedy Galleries Inc., New York

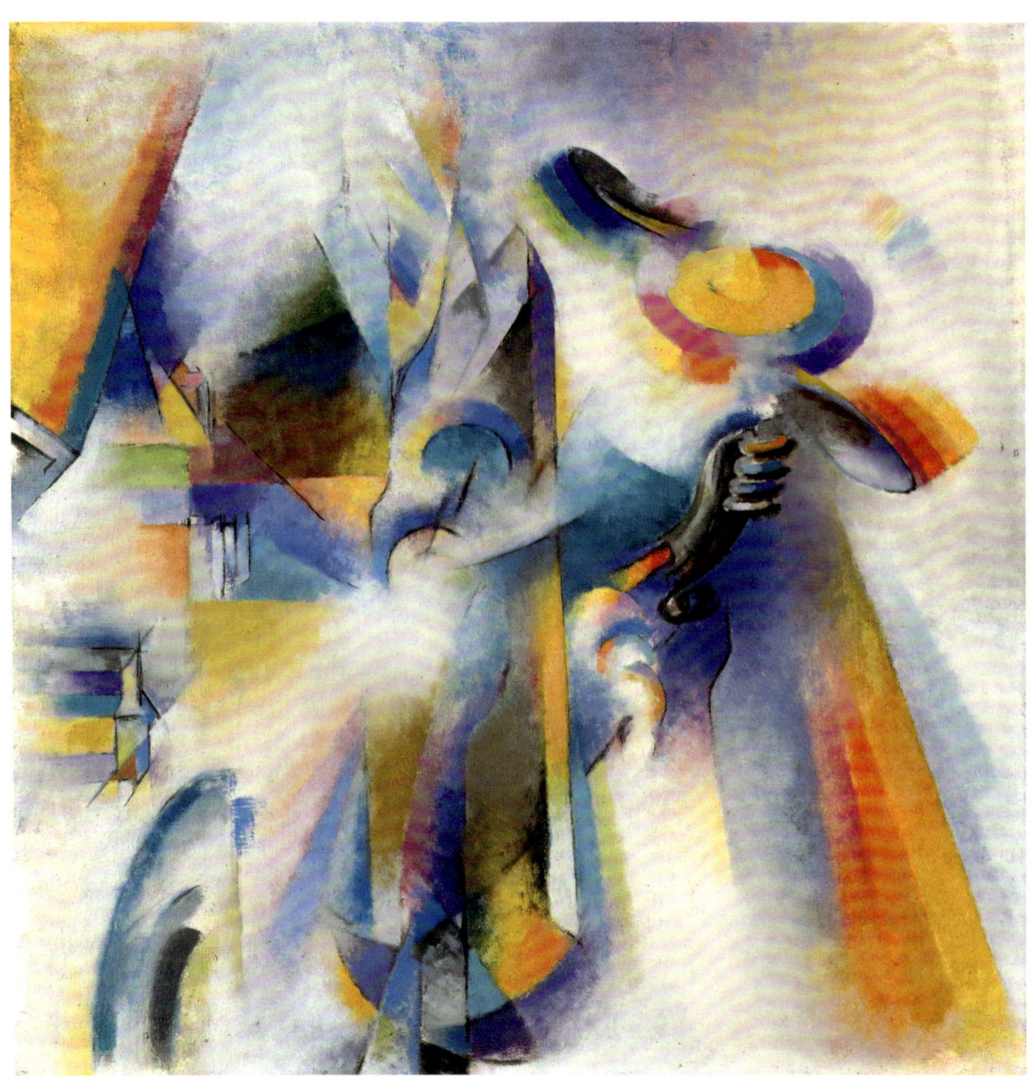

Stanton Macdonald-Wright

* *Aeroplane Synchromy in Yellow-Orange*, 1920, oil on canvas, 24 ¼ x 24″

Lent by The Metropolitan Museum of Art, Alfred Stieglitz Collection, 1949.

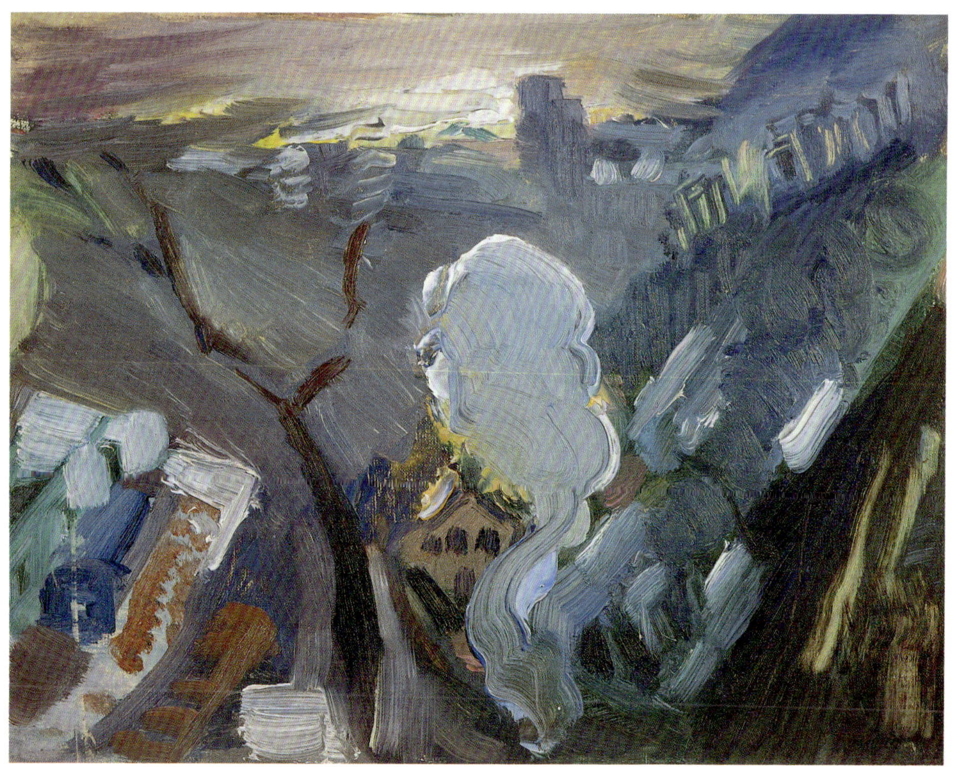

John Marin

Weehawken Sequence No. 5, 1903–4, oil on canvas mounted on composition board, 9 ½ x 12 ½″

Whitney Museum of American Art, Gift of Mr. and Mrs. John Marin, Jr.

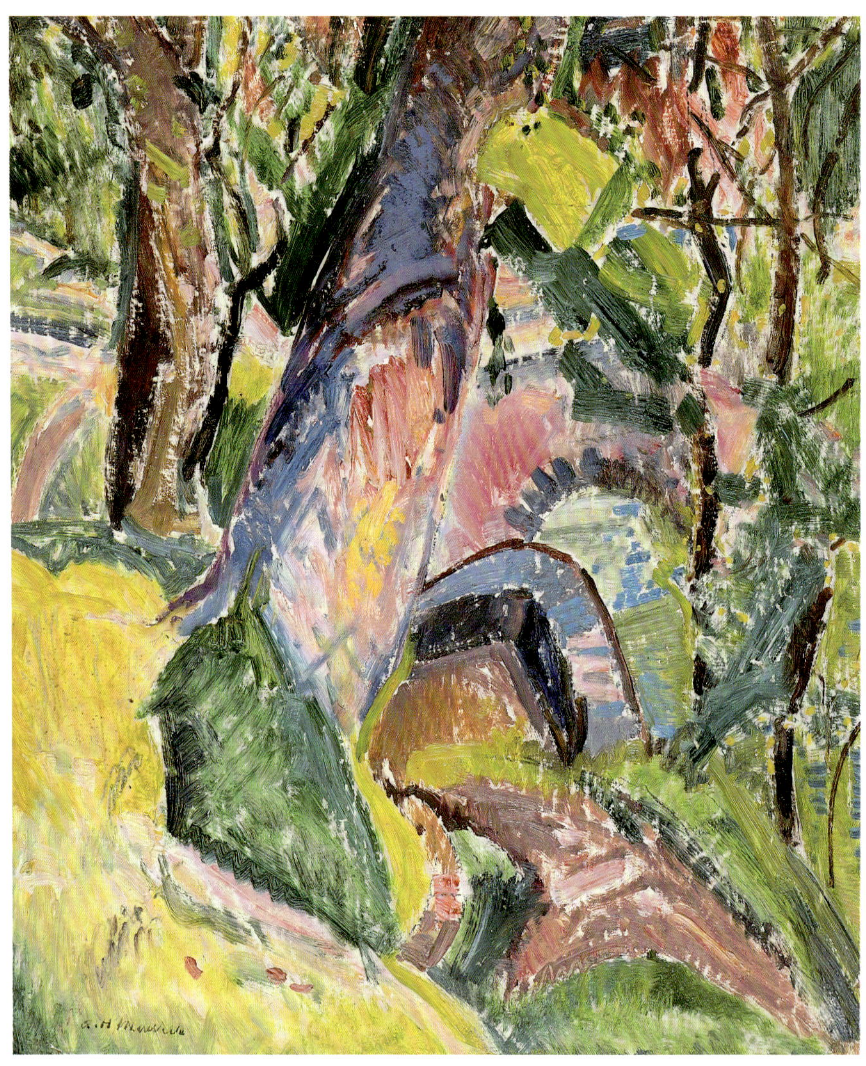

Alfred H. Maurer

Bridge Landscape No. 2, ca. 1916–18, oil on Upson board, 21¾ x 18″

Collection of Mr. and Mrs. Meyer P. Potamkin

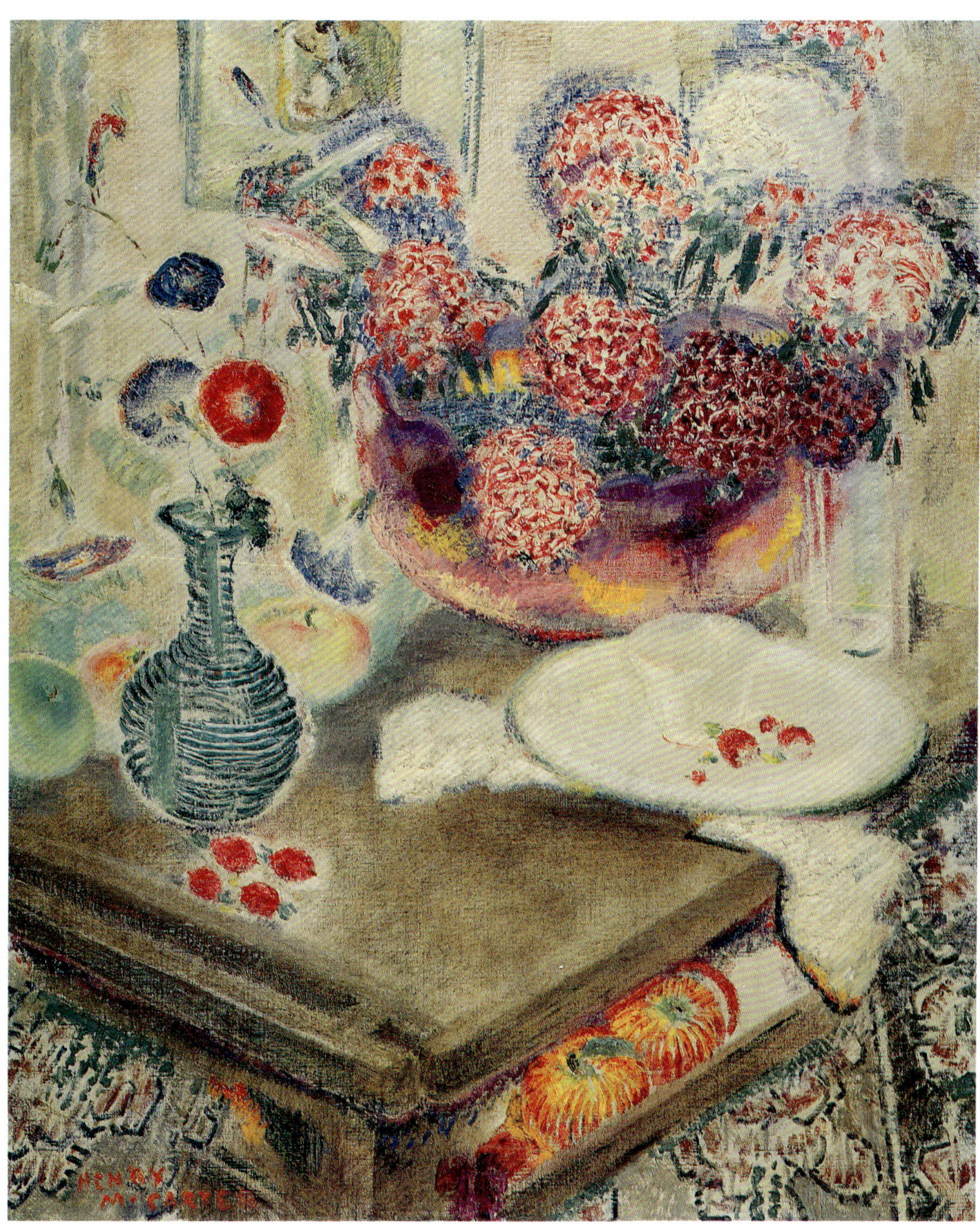

Henry McCarter

Flower Still Life, ca. 1920, oil on canvas, 35 15/16 x 29 15/16"
Museum of American Art of the Pennsylvania Academy of the Fine Arts. Gift of Mrs. George Roberts, 1975.4

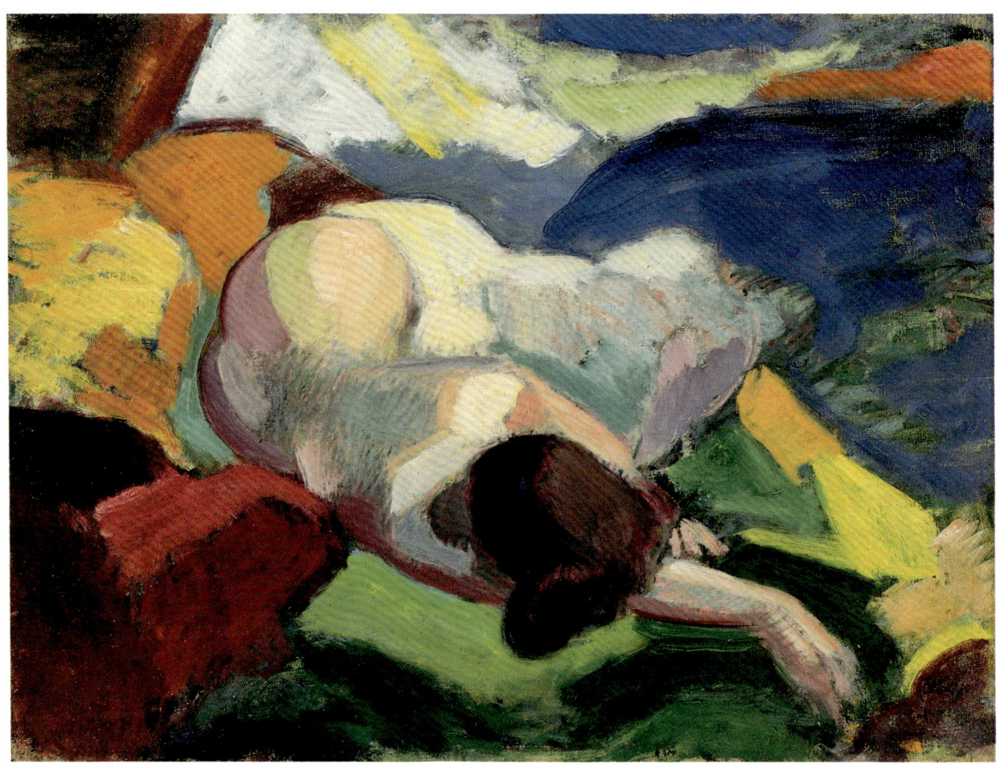

Carl Newman

Nude, ca. 1915–16, oil on canvas, 16 ⅛ x 22", National Museum of American Art, Smithsonian Institution, Gift of Anna McCleery Newton

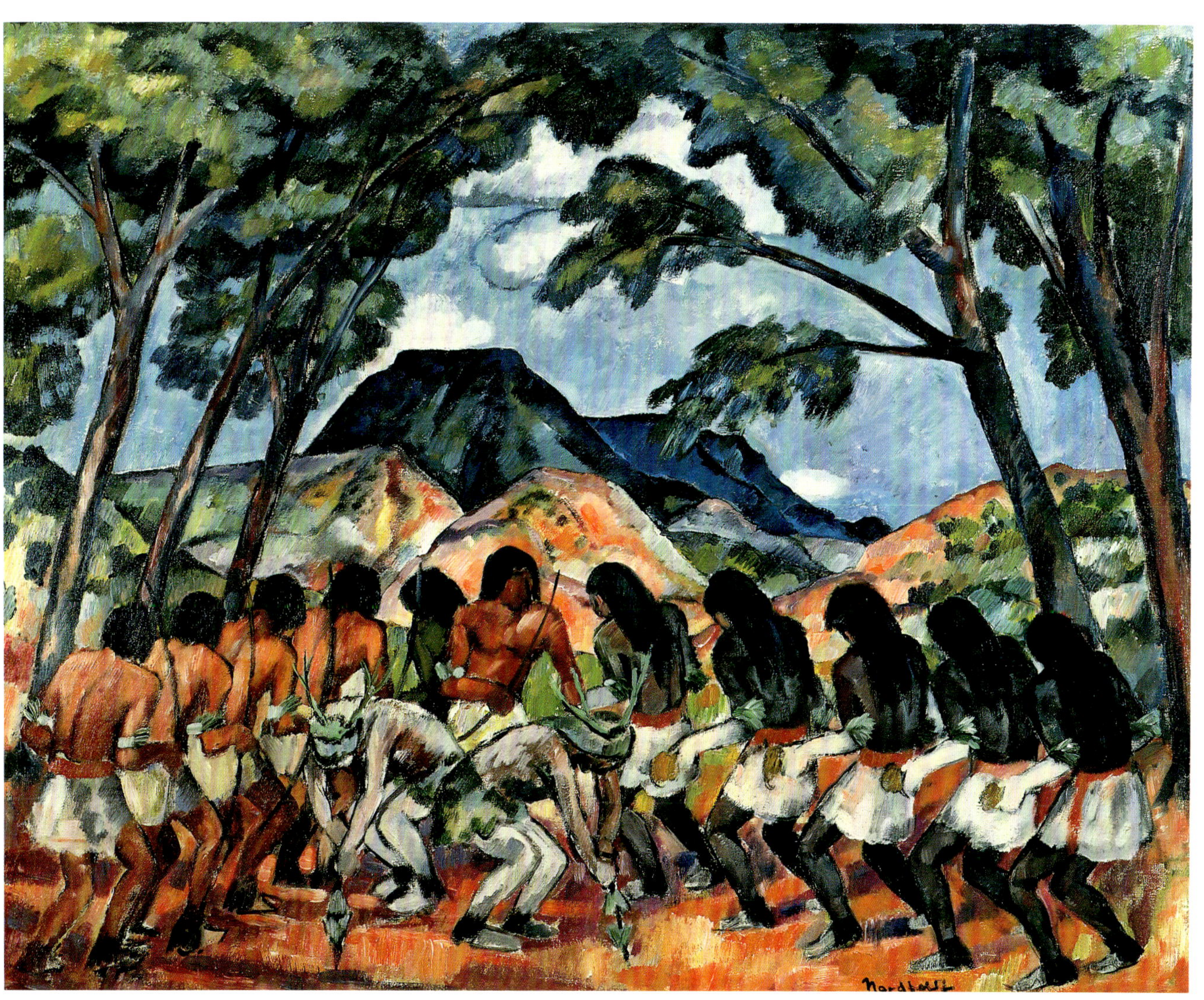

B. J. O. Nordfeldt

Antelope Dance, 1919, oil on canvas, 33⅝ x 43", Collection of the Museum of Fine Arts, Museum of New Mexico; Gift of Friends

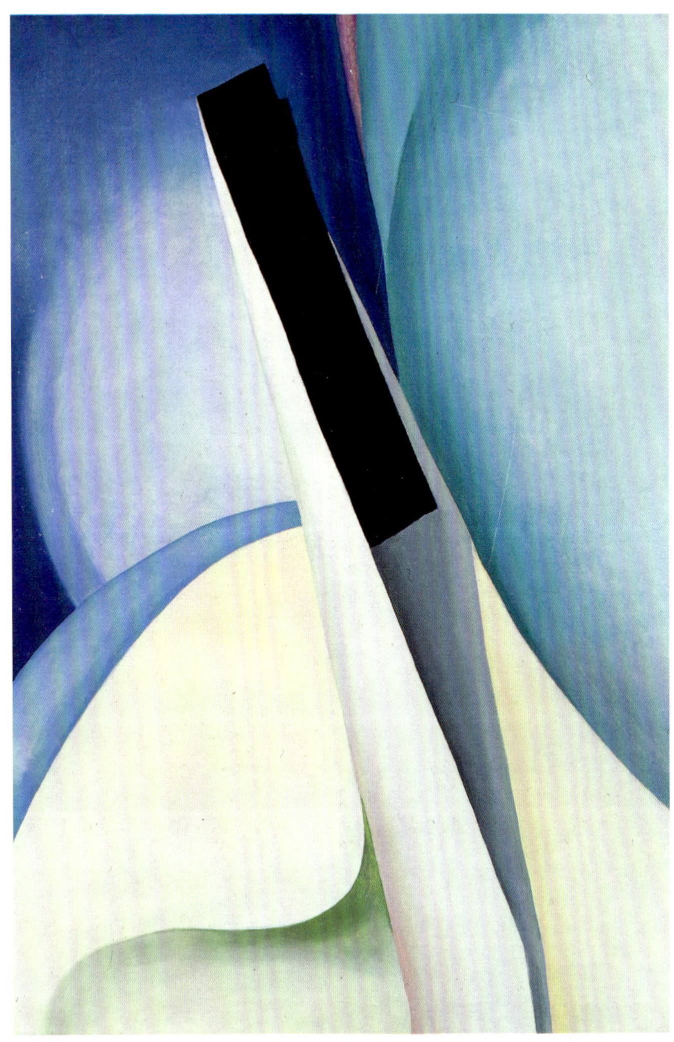

Georgia O'Keeffe

Black Spot No. 2, 1919, oil on canvas, 24 ¼ x 16 ¼"

Private collection

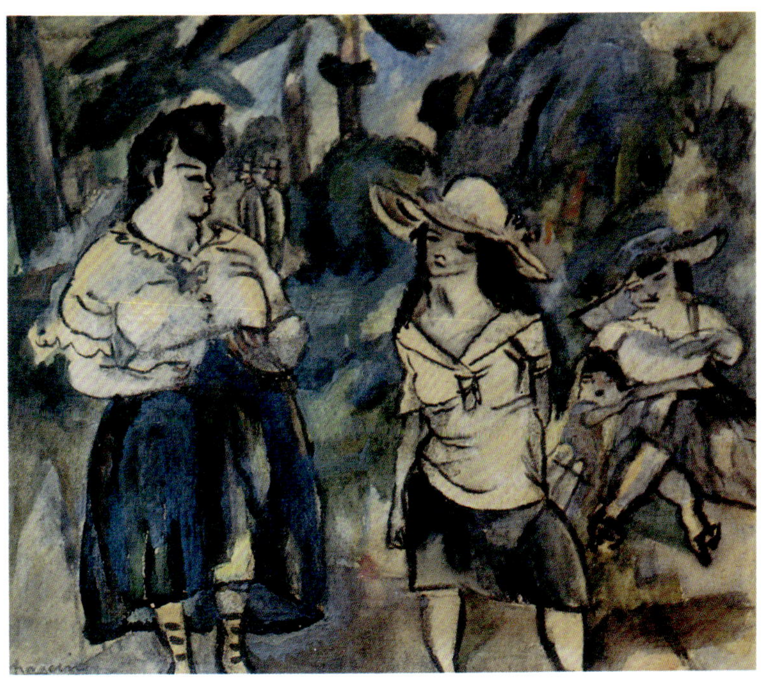

Jules Pascin

* *In a Park*, 1917, watercolor on paper, 6¼ x 7⅛"

Columbus Museum of Art, Ohio: Gift of Ferdinand Howald

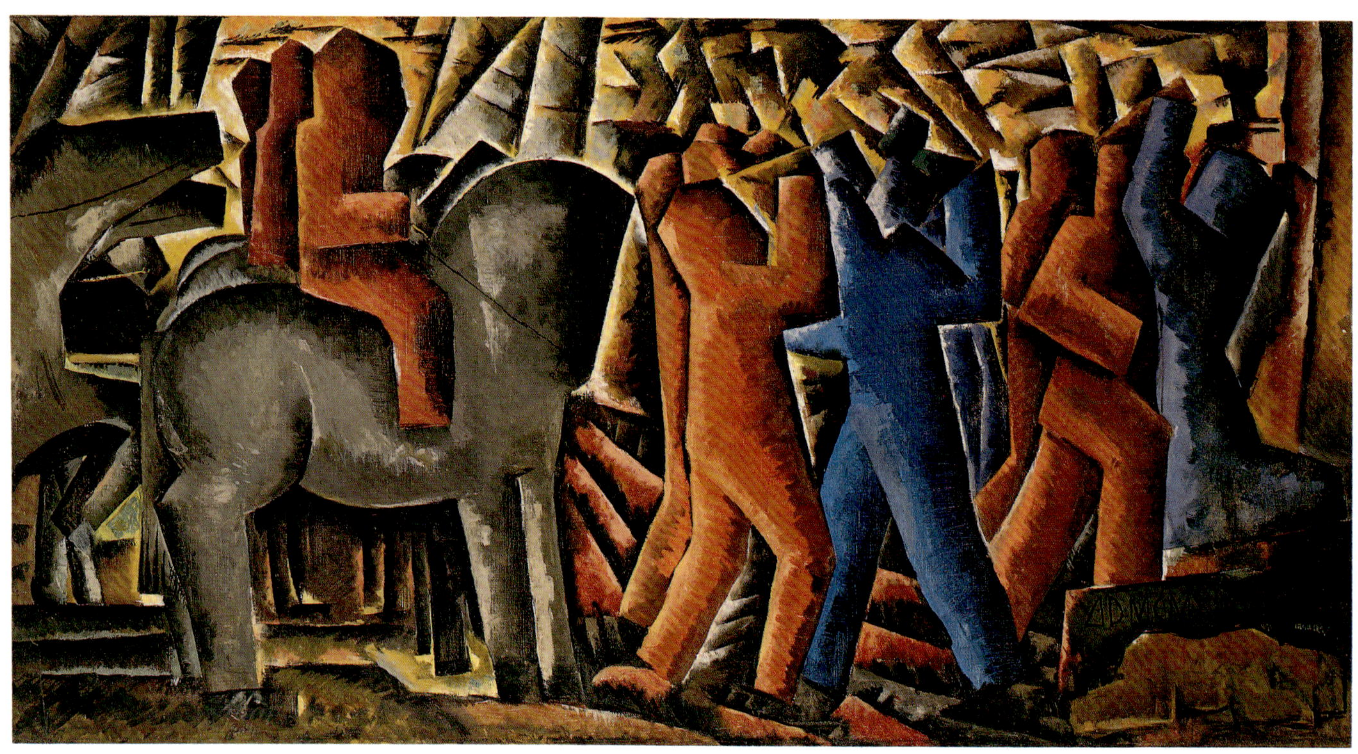

Man Ray

* *A.D. 1914*, 1914, oil on canvas, 36⅞ x 69¾"

Philadelphia Museum of Art, A.E. Gallatin Collection

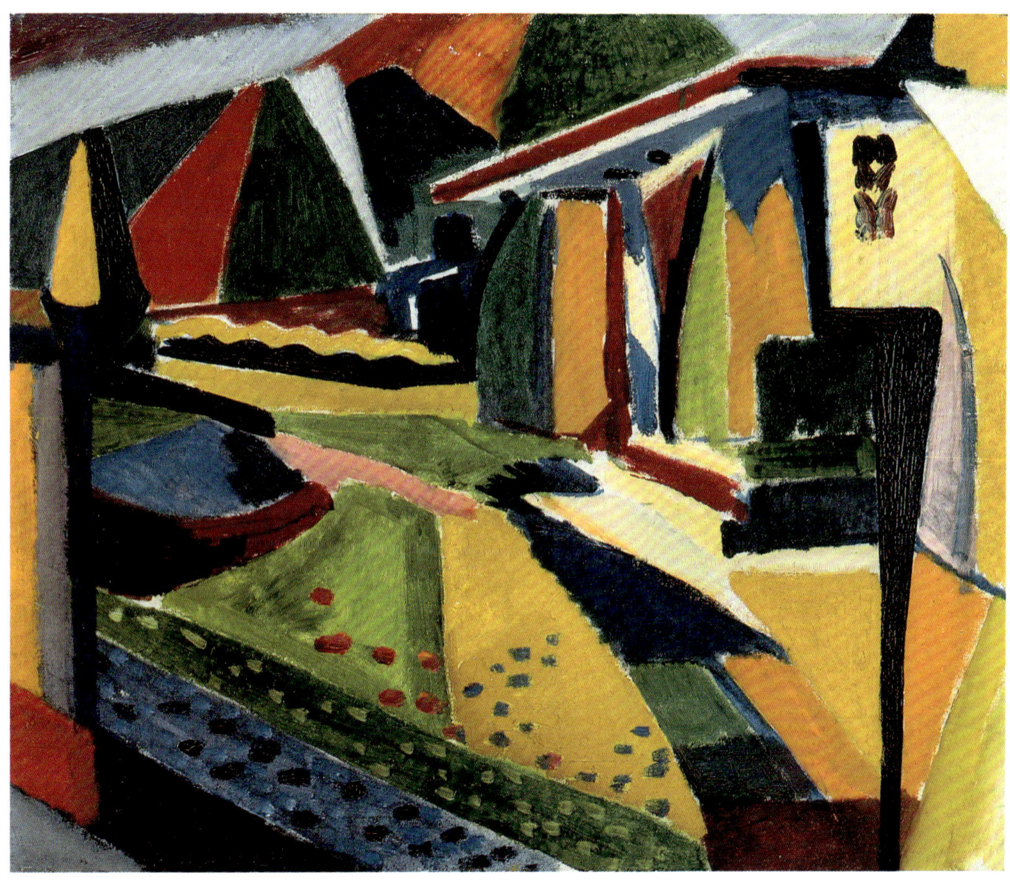

H. Lyman Saÿen

Abstract Landscape, 1915–16, oil on canvas, 25 x 30⅛″

National Museum of American Art, Smithsonian Institution,

Gift of H. Lyman Saÿen to his nation

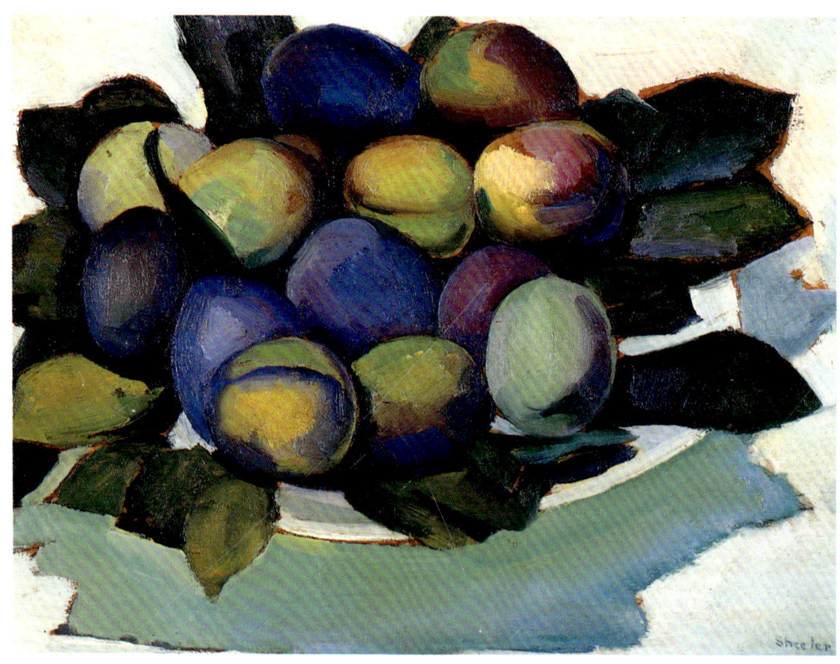

Charles Sheeler

Plums on a Plate, ca. 1910, oil on panel, 10½ x 14″

Collection of Mr. and Mrs. Meyer P. Potamkin

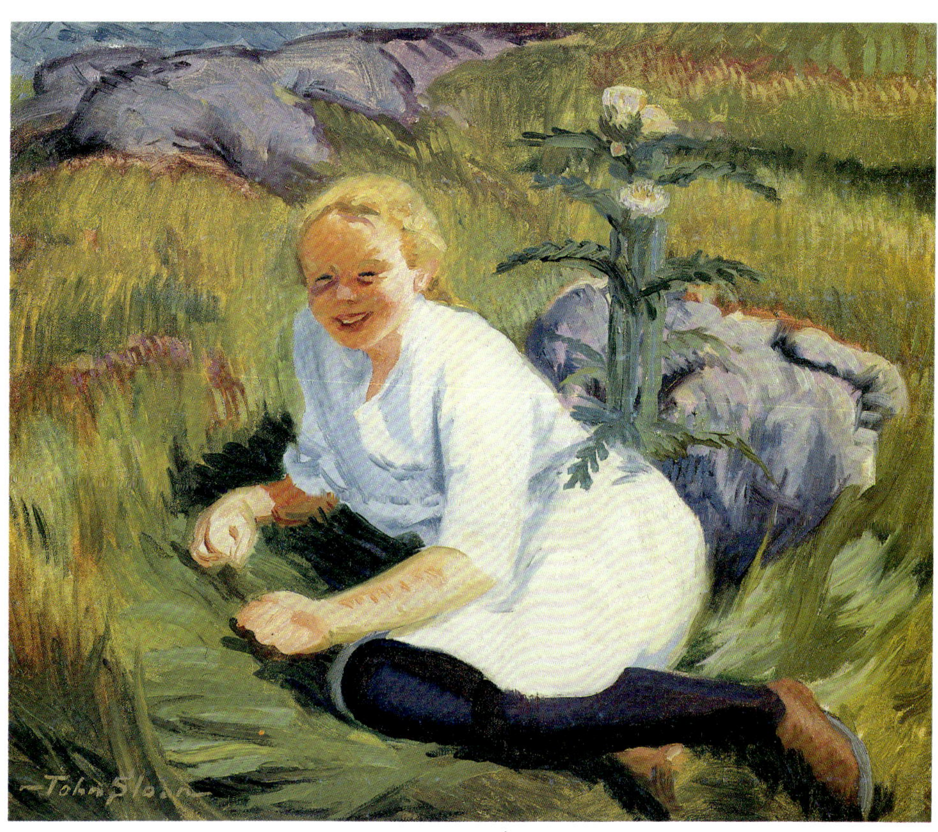

John Sloan

* *Child and Thistle in Sun*, 1916, oil on canvas, 20 x 24″

Courtesy of Kraushaar Galleries, New York

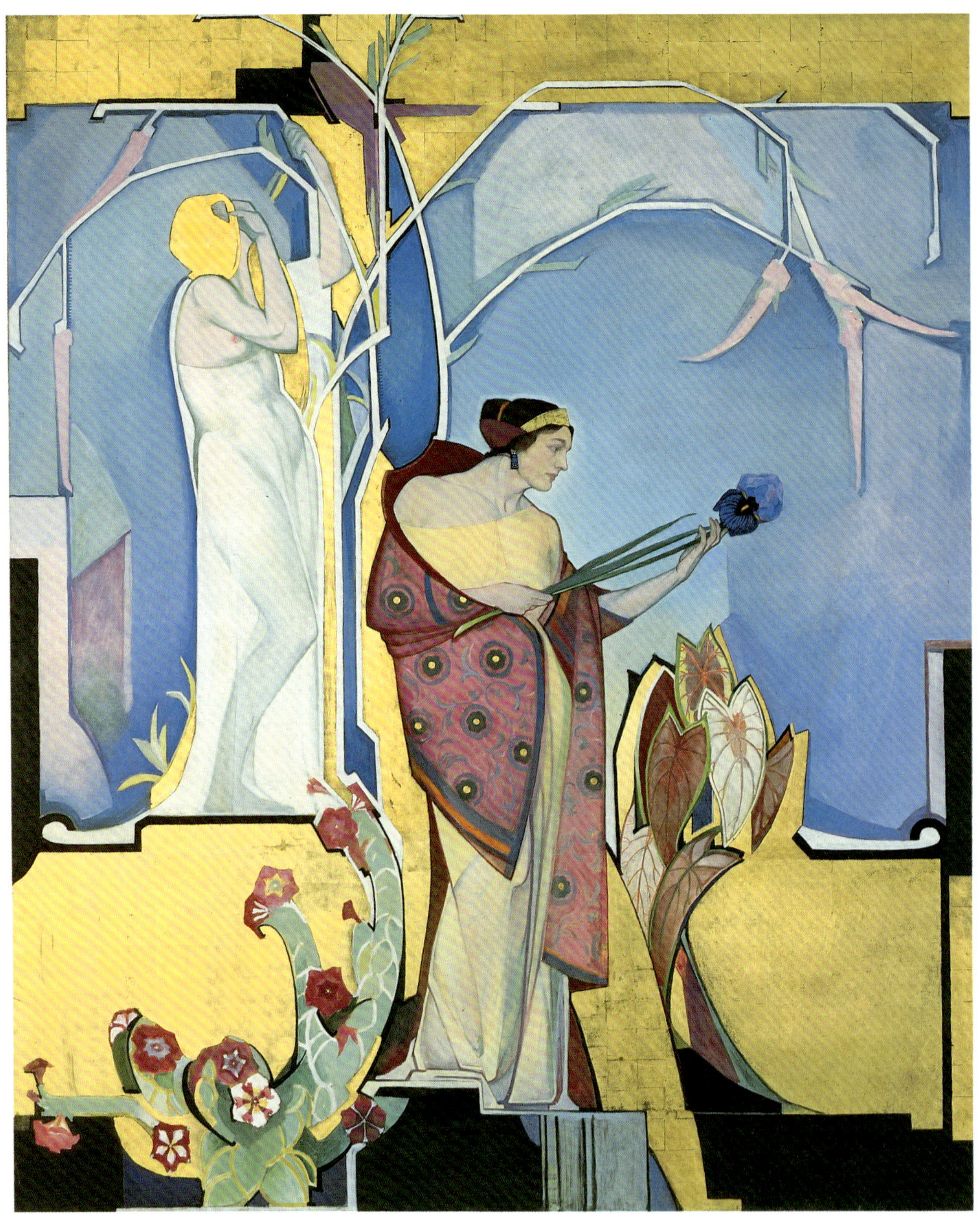

Edward J. Steichen

* *In Exaltation of Flowers: Petunia, Caladium, Budleya*, ca. 1910–13, tempera and gold leaf on canvas, 10′ x 8′4″
The Museum of Modern Art, New York, Gift of the Eugene and Agnes E. Meyer Collection, given by their family, 1974. Photograph ©1996 The Museum of Modern Art, New York

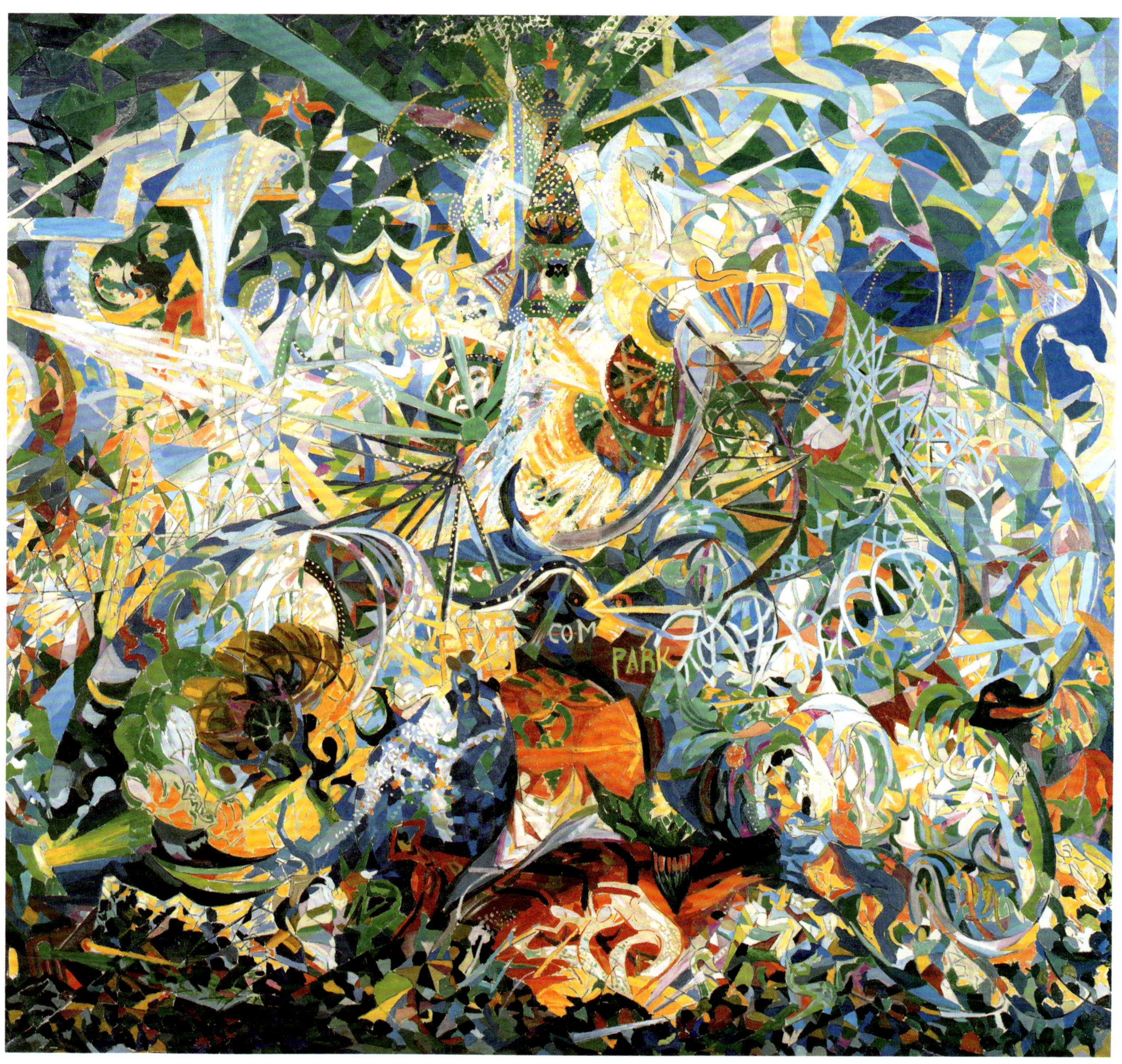

Joseph Stella

* *Battle of Lights, Coney Island, Mardi Gras*, 1913, oil on canvas, 75¾ x 84″

Yale University Art Gallery, Bequest of Dorothea Dreier to the Collection Société Anonyme

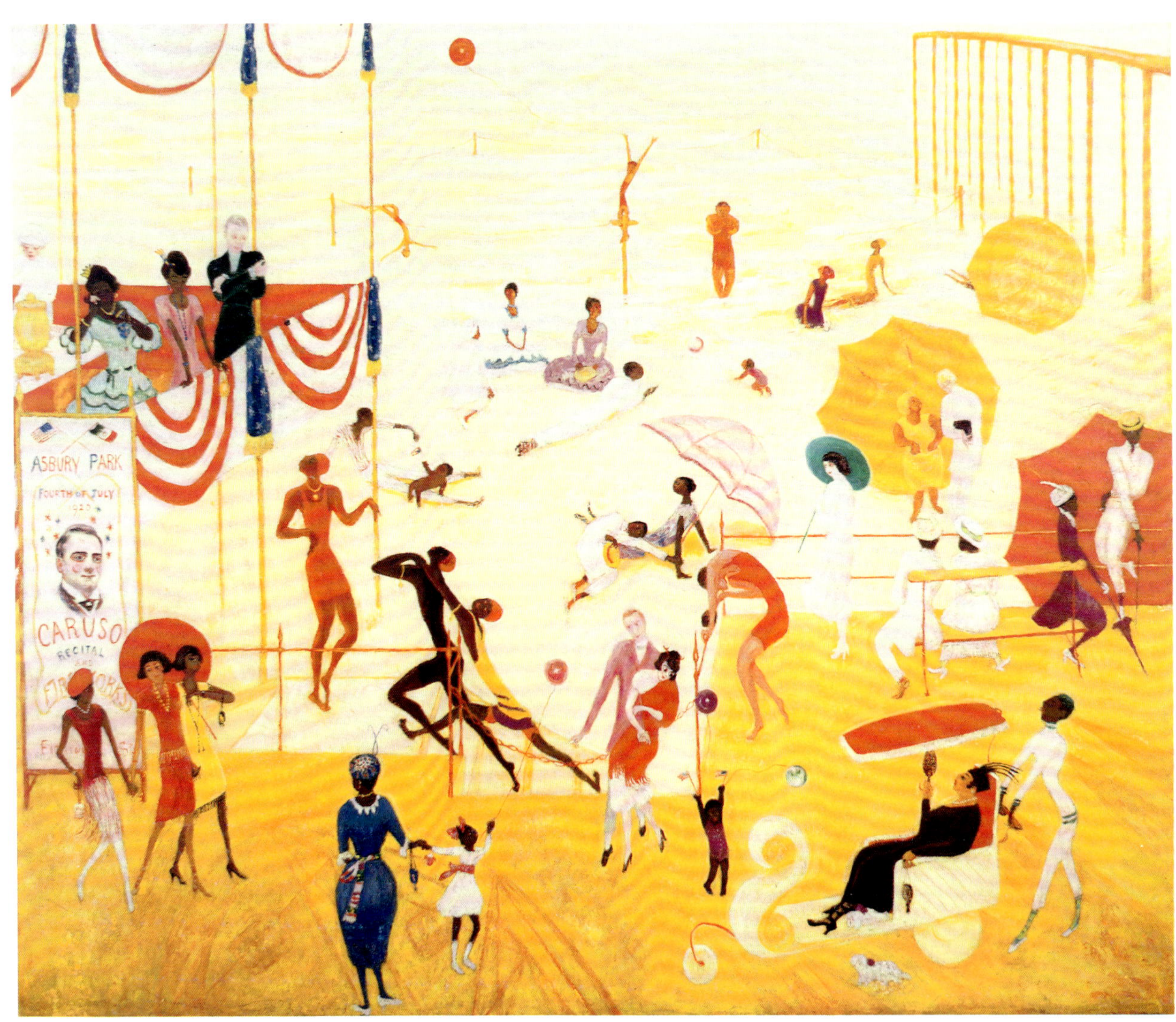

Florine Stettheimer

* *Asbury Park South*, 1920, oil on canvas, 50½ x 60½"

Collection Fisk University, Nashville, Tennessee, Gift of Carl Van Vechten

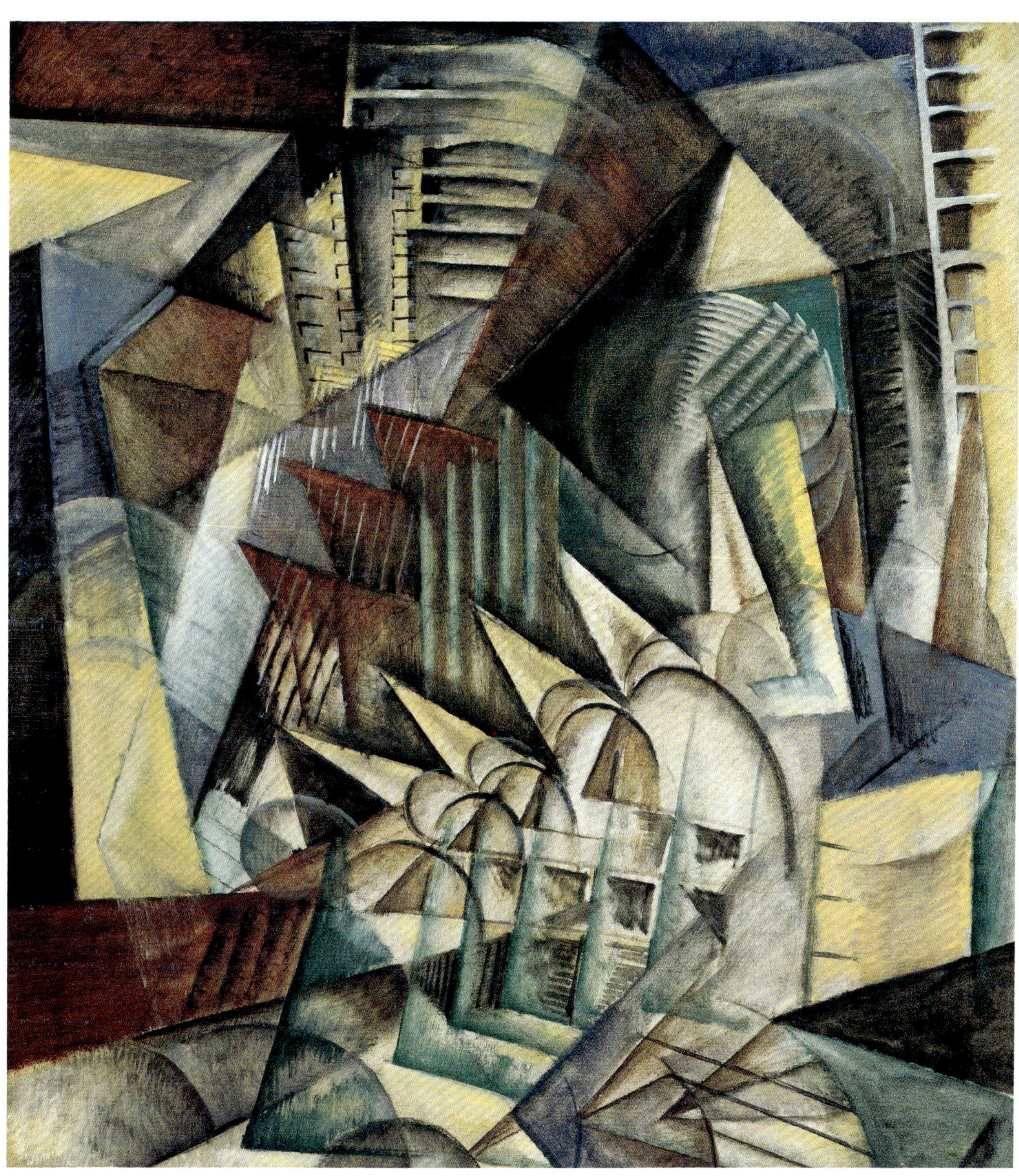

Max Weber

Rush Hour, New York, 1915, oil on canvas, 36¼ x 30¼"

National Gallery of Art, Washington, D.C., Gift of the Avalon Foundation

1970.6.1.

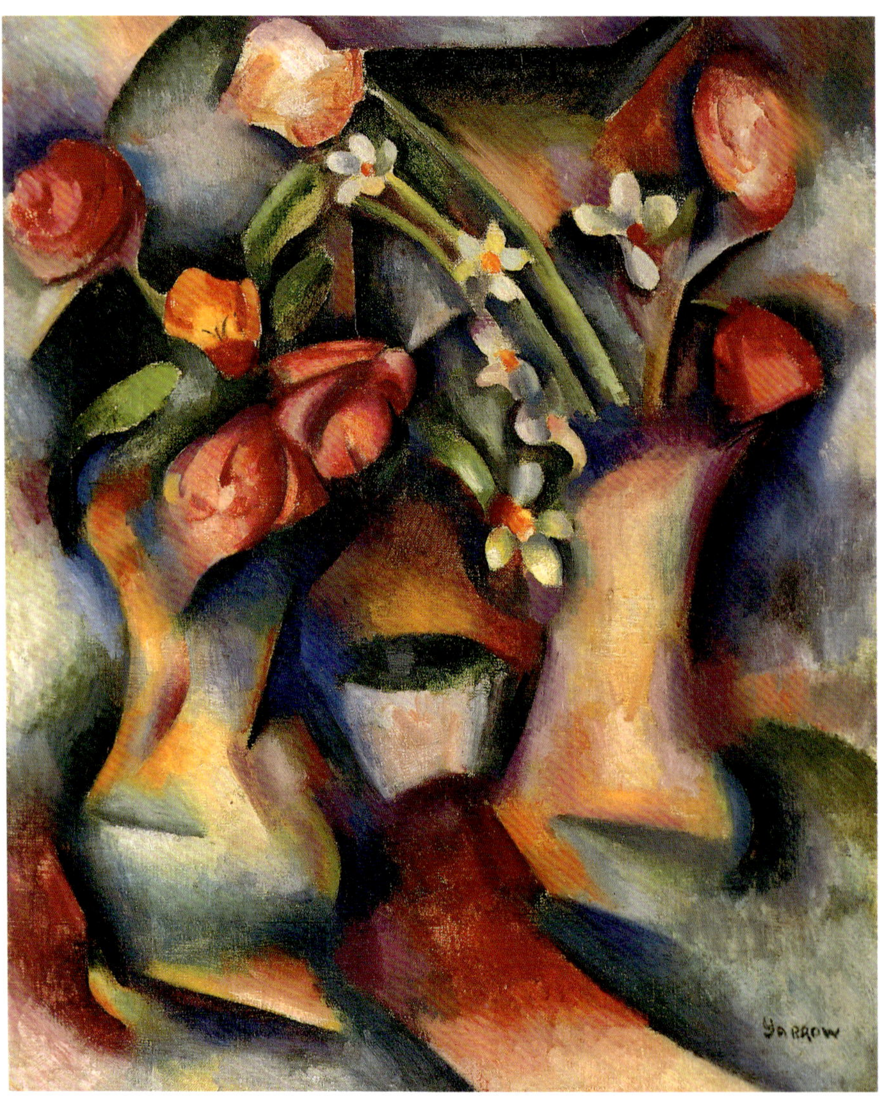

William H. K. Yarrow

* *Flowers*, ca. 1920, oil on canvas, 30 x 24″

Collection of Ellen Speiser Katz

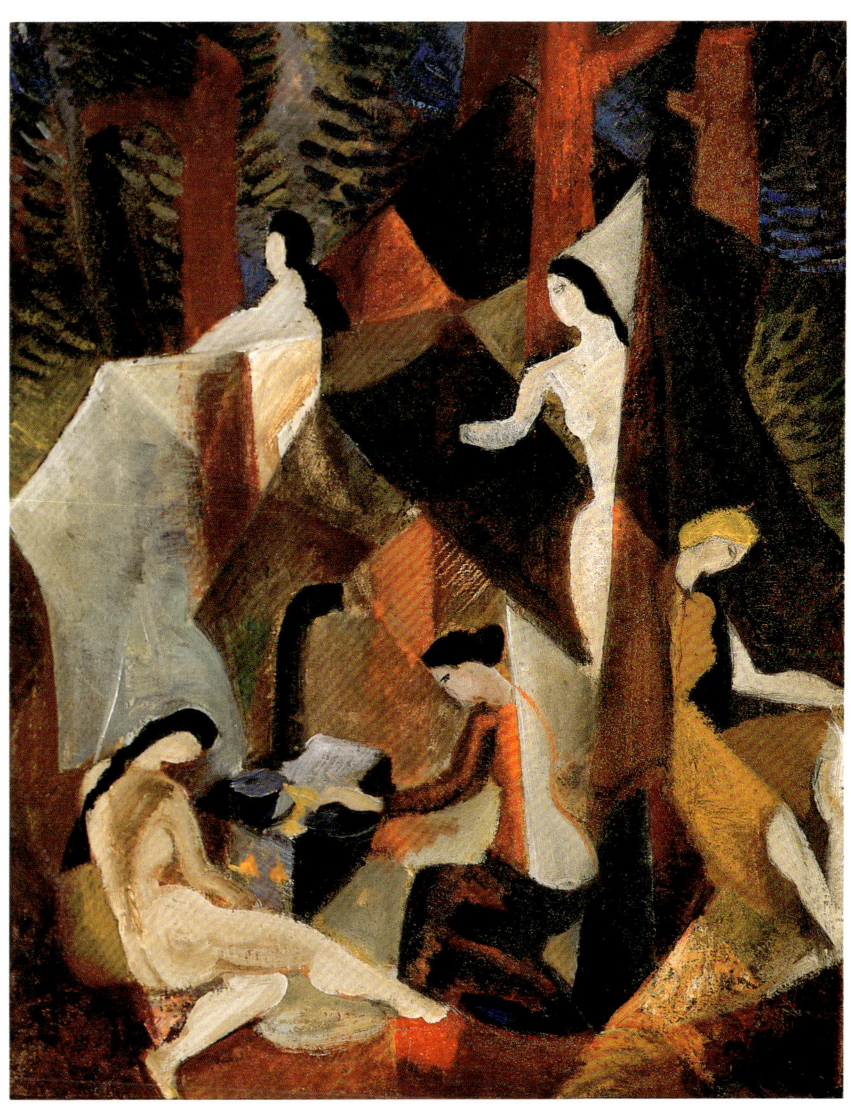

Marguerite Zorach

* *Camp in the Woods*, 1920, oil on canvas, 20 x 16"

Collection of Mr. and Mrs. Irwin L. Bernstein

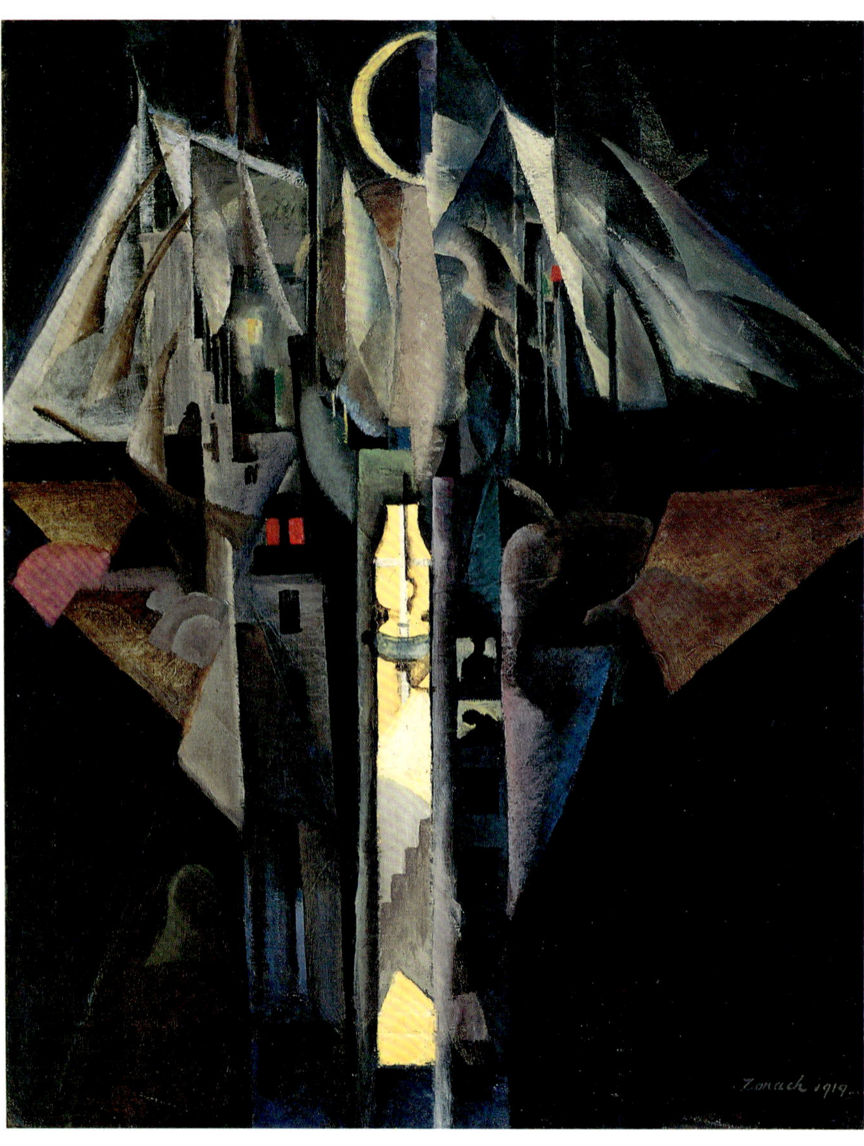

William Zorach

* *Mirage—Ships at Night*, 1919, oil on canvas, 32½ x 26"
National Museum of American Art, Smithsonian Institution,
Gift from the collection of the Zorach children

TO BE MODERN
EXHIBITION CHECKLIST

• Included in "Exhibition of Paintings and Drawings Showing the Later Tendencies in Art," April 16–May 15, 1921, Pennsylvania Academy of the Fine Arts

Ben Benn (1884–1983)
Staten Island Landscape, New York, 1918
Oil on canvas
19¾ x 15¾"
Collection of Mr. and Mrs. Meyer P. Potamkin

Ben Benn (1884–1983)
Woman with Velvet Hat, 1926
Oil on canvas
21 x 16¼"
Collection of Mr. and Mrs. Meyer P. Potamkin

Thomas Hart Benton (1889–1975)
Flowers, 1912
Watercolor over traces of graphite underdrawing on paper
17¾ x 13⅓"
Philadelphia Museum of Art, The Samuel S. White, III, and Vera White Collection

Thomas Hart Benton (1889–1975)
The Cliffs, 1921
Oil on canvas
29 x 34⅝"
Hirshhorn Museum and Sculpture Garden, Smithsonian Institution. Gift of Joseph H. Hirshhorn, 1966

George Biddle (1885–1973)
Tahitians, ca. 1920
Oil on canvas
60 x 50 1/16"
Museum of American Art of the Pennsylvania Academy of the Fine Arts. John Lambert Fund, 1921.3

George Biddle (1885–1973)
Three Nudes, 1921
Lithograph on cream-colored paper
6⅝ x 10"
Museum of American Art of the Pennsylvania Academy of the Fine Arts. Gift of the artist, 1960.23.81

Louis Bouché (1896–1969)
Still Life, 1920
Oil on canvas
24 x 20"
Courtesy of Kraushaar Galleries, New York

Paul Burlin (1886–1969)
Figure Sketch, 1921
Ink, pastel, and graphite on paper
13 5/16 x 9"
Whitney Museum of American Art, Gift of Gertrude Vanderbilt Whitney

Paul Burlin (1886–1969)
The Paddock, ca. 1921–24
Oil on canvas
19¾ x 28¾"
Collection of The Newark Museum, Purchase 1945 Thomas L. Raymond Bequest Fund and Endowment Interest Fund

Arthur B. Carles (1882–1952)
Flowers, 1914
Monoprint with pastel on paper
20 x 17"
Collection of Perry and June Ottenberg

Arthur B. Carles (1882–1952)
• *Profile (Gardenia),* 1921
Oil on canvas
30 x 24"
Courtesy of Mr. and Mrs. Philip Sherman

Sara Carles (1894–1965)
In White, ca. 1923
Oil on canvas
30 1/16 x 25 1/16"
Museum of American Art of the Pennsylvania Academy of the Fine Arts. John Lambert Fund, 1924.1

John Covert (1882–1960)
• *Temptation of Saint Anthony,* 1916
Oil on canvas
25 11/16 x 23¾"
Yale University Art Gallery, Gift of Collection Société Anonyme

e.e. cummings (1894–1962)
A Drawing (Elephant)
The Dial 70 (January 1921)
9½ x 6½"
Temple University Libraries

Andrew Dasburg (1887–1979)
Apples, 1920
Oil on canvas
16 x 24¼"
Whitney Museum of American Art, Purchase

Andrew Dasburg (1887–1979)
Landscape, 1920
Graphite on paper
12 7/16 x 15½"
Whitney Museum of American Art, Gift of Gertrude Vanderbilt Whitney

Arthur B. Davies (1862–1928)
• *Three Masks,* ca. 1920
Oil on canvas
28 x 23"
Collection Denver Art Museum. Museum purchase

Arthur B. Davies (1862–1928)
Valkyries, 1920
Aquatint, sugar lift, roulette, and plate tone on blue laid paper
10½ x 15⅝
Museum of American Art of the Pennsylvania Academy of the Fine Arts. John S. Phillips Fund, 1990.14.7

Charles Demuth (1883–1935)
Vaudeville Dancers, 1916–18
Black watercolor over graphite on off-white laid paper
8⅛ x 11⅝"
Museum of American Art of the Pennsylvania Academy of the Fine Arts. Gift of Mrs. Margot Newman Stickley in memory of her parents, Philip and Hélène S. Newman, 1987.18.1

Charles Demuth (1883–1935)
A Box of Tricks, 1919
Gouache and graphite on cardboard
19⅞ x 15⅞"
Museum of American Art of the Pennsylvania Academy of the Fine Arts. Acquired from the Philadelphia Museum of Art in partial exchange for the John S. Phillips Collection of European drawings, 1984.4

Charles Demuth (1883–1935)
• *Aucassin and Nicolette,* 1921
Oil on canvas
24⅛ x 20"
Columbus Museum of Art, Ohio: Gift of Ferdinand Howald

Charles Demuth (1883–1935)
• *From the Garden of the Château,* 1921
Oil on canvas
25 x 20"
The Fine Arts Museums of San Francisco, Museum purchase, Roscoe and Margaret Oakes Income Fund, Ednah Root, and the Walter H. and Phyllis J. Shorenstein Fund, 1990.4

Marius de Zayas (1880–1961)
• *John Marin and Alfred Stieglitz,* ca. 1912
Charcoal on paper
24¼ x 18⅝"
Lent by The Metropolitan Museum of Art, Alfred Stieglitz Collection, 1949

Marius de Zayas (1880–1961)
• *Katharine N. Rhoades,* ca. 1915
Charcoal on paper
23⅞ x 17⅝"
Lent by The Metropolitan Museum of Art, Alfred Stieglitz Collection, 1949

Preston Dickinson (1891–1930)
Café Scene (Portrait of Charles Demuth), ca. 1912–14
Charcoal and black chalk on tan wove paper
18 x 13¾"
Collection of Mr. and Mrs. Meyer P. Potamkin

Preston Dickinson (1891–1930)
Village by the Sea, ca. 1918
Oil on canvas
12 x 16"
Collection of Mr. and Mrs. Meyer P. Potamkin

Preston Dickinson (1891–1930)
• *Factories,* 1920
Pencil and gouache on paper
14 x 20¼"
Collection of The Newark Museum, Gift of Ruth, Rachel, and Toby Armour in memory of their father, Bernard R. Armour, 1955

Arthur G. Dove (1880–1946)
• *League of Nations,* ca. 1914
Pastel on thin paper, mounted on pulp board
21 5/16 x 17 13/16"
Georgia Museum of Art, University of Georgia; Eva Underhill Holbrook Memorial Collection of American Art, gift of Alfred Heber Holbrook. GMOA 45.32

Katherine S. Dreier (1877–1952)
Self-Portrait, 1911
Oil on canvas
20 x 16"
Yale University Art Gallery, Bequest of Katherine S. Dreier to the Collection Société Anonyme

William Glackens (1870–1938)
At the Beach, ca. 1918
Oil on canvas
25 x 30"
Collection of The Newark Museum, Gift of Mrs. Felix Fuld, 1925

William Glackens (1870–1938)
• *Finnish Woman,* 1920
Oil on canvas
32 x 26"
Courtesy of Kraushaar Galleries, New York

Bernard Gussow (1881–1957)
Untitled
Oil on canvas
30 x 25¼"
The Montclair Art Museum, Gift of Dr. and Mrs. Milton Luria

Bernard Gussow (1881–1957)
Untitled, ca. 1915
Watercolor on paper
10½ x 16⅛″
The Montclair Art Museum,
Gift of Dr. and Mrs. Milton Luria

Samuel Halpert (1884–1930)
Southern France, 1914
Oil on canvas
25¼ x 31⅛″
Georgia Museum of Art, University of Georgia; gift of Edith Gregor Halpert. GMOA 46.143

Samuel Halpert (1884–1930)
Through the Window, 1918
Oil on canvas
20¼ x 16″
The Phillips Collection,
Washington, D.C.

Marsden Hartley (1877–1943)
Movement: Provincetown, 1916
Oil over carbon pencil on panel
20 x 15¾″
Collection of Mr. and Mrs. Meyer P. Potamkin

Marsden Hartley (1877–1943)
Vase of Flowers, 1917
Oil on glass
13⅜ x 9″
Alfred Stieglitz Collection of Modern Art, Fisk University, Nashville, Tennessee

Marsden Hartley (1877–1943)
New Mexico Landscape, 1919
Oil on canvas
17⅞ x 26″
Philadelphia Museum of Art,
The Alfred Stieglitz Collection

Marsden Hartley (1877–1943)
Near Aix-en-Provence, 1928
Ink and carbon pencil on paper
28⅛ x 21⅛″
Collection of Mr. and Mrs. Meyer P. Potamkin

Morris Kantor (1896–1974)
Self-Portrait, 1918
Oil on linen
22⅛ x 18″
National Museum of American Art, Smithsonian Institution, Gift of Mrs. Morris Kantor

Walt Kuhn (1877–1949)
The Tragic Comedians, ca. 1916
Oil on canvas
96 x 45″
Hirshhorn Museum and Sculpture Garden, Smithsonian Institution. Gift of Joseph H. Hirshhorn, 1966

Walt Kuhn (1877–1949)
• *The City*, 1919
Oil on canvas
89 x 52″
Courtesy of Kennedy Galleries Inc., New York

Yasuo Kuniyoshi (1893–1953)
Landscape, ca. 1919
Oil on panel
8¼ x 10⅜″
Philadelphia Museum of Art,
Gift of Frank and Alice Osborn

Yasuo Kuniyoshi (1893–1953)
Maine Family, ca. 1922–23
Oil on canvas
30 x 24″
The Phillips Collection, Washington, D.C.

Robert Laurent (1890–1970)
Rocks in a Landscape, 1920
Charcoal on paper
14⅞ x 19¾″
Courtesy of Kraushaar Galleries, New York

Stanton Macdonald-Wright
(1890–1973)
• *Aeroplane Synchromy in Yellow-Orange*, 1920
Oil on canvas
24¼ x 24″
Lent by The Metropolitan Museum of Art, Alfred Stieglitz Collection, 1949

John Marin (1870–1953)
Weehawken Sequence No. 5, 1903–4
Oil on canvas mounted on composition board
9½ x 12½″
Whitney Museum of American Art,
Gift of Mr. and Mrs. John Marin, Jr.

John Marin (1870–1953)
From the Window of "291," Looking Down Fifth Avenue, 1911
Watercolor and pencil on paper
16⅜ x 13⅜″
Lent by The Metropolitan Museum of Art, Alfred Stieglitz Collection, 1949

John Marin (1870–1953)
Sun, Sea, Land—Maine, 1921
Watercolor over charcoal on heavy off-white wove paper
16½ x 19 7/16″
Museum of American Art of the Pennsylvania Academy of the Fine Arts. John S. Phillips Bequest, 1876 (By exchange: acquired from the Samuel S. White, III, and Vera White Collection, given to the Philadelphia Museum of Art in 1967), 1985.21

Alfred H. Maurer (1868–1932)
Bridge Landscape No. 2, ca. 1916–18
Oil on Upson board
21¾ x 18″
Collection of Mr. and Mrs. Meyer P. Potamkin

Alfred H. Maurer (1868–1932)
Head, ca. 1920
Oil on composition board
21⅝ x 11½″
Collection of The Newark Museum, Gift of Dr. and Mrs. Charles F. Gibbs, 1977

Alfred H. Maurer (1868–1932)
Portrait of a Girl, ca. 1920
Watercolor on paper
21½ x 18″
Courtesy of Kraushaar Galleries, New York

Henry McCarter (1864–1942)
Symphony, by 1915
Oil on canvas
103⅜ x 100⅜″
Museum of American Art of the Pennsylvania Academy of the Fine Arts. Gift of Mrs. Henry Clifford, 1944.33

Henry McCarter (1864–1942)
Flower Still Life, ca. 1920
Oil on canvas
35 15/16 x 29 15/16″
Museum of American Art of the Pennsylvania Academy of the Fine Arts. Gift of Mrs. George Roberts, 1975.4

Carl Newman (1858–1932)
Landscape, ca. 1915
Oil on canvas
25⅛ x 30⅛″
Philadelphia Museum of Art, Gift of Dr. and Mrs. Milton Luria in memory of Mr. and Mrs. Samuel Herman

Carl Newman (1858–1932)
Nude, ca. 1915–16
Oil on canvas
16⅛ x 22″
National Museum of American Art, Smithsonian Institution, Gift of Anna McCleery Newton

B. J. O. Nordfeldt (1887–1955)
Antelope Dance, 1919
Oil on canvas
33⅜ x 43″
Collection of the Museum of Fine Arts, Museum of New Mexico; Gift of Friends

Georgia O'Keeffe (1887–1986)
Untitled, 1915–16
Charcoal on paper
24¼ x 18¾″
The Georgia O'Keeffe Foundation

Georgia O'Keeffe (1887–1986)
Black Spot No. 2, 1919
Oil on canvas
24¼ x 16¼″
Private collection

Georgia O'Keeffe (1887–1986)
Orange and Red Streak, 1919
Oil on canvas
27 x 23″
Philadelphia Museum of Art, Bequest of Georgia O'Keeffe for the Alfred Stieglitz Collection

Georgia O'Keeffe (1887–1986)
Green Apple on Black Plate, ca. 1921
Oil on canvas
14⅛ x 12⅛″
Collection of the Birmingham Museum of Art, Birmingham, Alabama; Museum purchase with funds provided by the 1981–82 Beaux Arts Committee, Museum Store, and donors

Walter Pach (1883–1958)
Landscape, 1914
Watercolor over traces of graphite underdrawing on paper
9⅞ x 14⅛″
Philadelphia Museum of Art,
The Louise and Walter Arensberg Collection

Jules Pascin (1885–1930)
• *In a Park*, 1917
Watercolor on paper
6¼ x 7⅛″
Columbus Museum of Art, Ohio:
Gift of Ferdinand Howald

Jules Pascin (1885–1930)
Seated Girl with Bouquet, 1921–22
Oil on canvas
35½ x 28¾″
Collection of Mr. and Mrs. Meyer P. Potamkin

Man Ray (1890–1976)
• *A.D. 1914*, 1914
Oil on canvas
36⅞ x 69¾″
Philadelphia Museum of Art, A. E. Gallatin Collection

H. Lyman Saÿen (1875–1918)
Abstract Landscape, 1915–16
Oil on canvas
25 x 30⅛″
National Museum of American Art, Smithsonian Institution, Gift of H. Lyman Saÿen to his nation

H. Lyman Saÿen (1875–1918)
Fir Trees, 1915–16
Oil on canvas
25 x 30″
Philadelphia Museum of Art, Gift of the National Collection of Fine Arts

Morton L. Schamberg (1881–1918)
View from the Side Boxes (Opera), ca. 1910–11
Pastel on board
5½ x 7¼″
Museum of American Art of the Pennsylvania Academy of the Fine Arts. Purchased with funds from the Joseph E. Temple Fund, Mrs. Robert P. Levy, Mrs. Kenneth W. Gemmill, and Frank and Betsy Goodyear, 1982.4

Morton L. Schamberg (1881–1918)
Landscape, Bridge, 1915
Oil on panel
13¾ x 10″
Philadelphia Museum of Art, Gift of Dr. and Mrs. Ira Leo Schamberg

Morton L. Schamberg (1881–1918)
Painting IV (Mechanical Abstraction), 1916
Oil on panel
13¾ x 10¾″
Philadelphia Museum of Art, The Louise and Walter Arensberg Collection

Charles Sheeler (1883–1965)
Plums on a Plate, ca. 1910
Oil on panel
10½x 14″
Collection of Mr. and Mrs. Meyer P. Potamkin

Charles Sheeler (1883–1965)
Bucks County Barn, 1918
Opaque watercolor and black chalk on paper
10¼ x 13¾″
Philadelphia Museum of Art, A. E. Gallatin Collection

John Sloan (1871–1951)
Fifth Avenue Critics, 1905
Etching on buff wove paper
4 9/16 x 6⅝″
Museum of American Art of the Pennsylvania Academy of the Fine Arts. Gift of Mr. H. Lea Hudson, 1972.11.1

John Sloan (1871–1951)
Hot Summer, City Apartment, ca. 1905
Litho crayon on cream wove paper
9⅜ x 12″
Museum of American Art of the Pennsylvania Academy of the Fine Arts. Gift of Mr. and Mrs. Rowland Elzea, 1978.8.2

John Sloan (1871–1951)
• *Child and Thistle in Sun*, 1916
Oil on canvas
20 x 24″
Courtesy of Kraushaar Galleries, New York

Edward J. Steichen (1879–1973)
• *In Exaltation of Flowers: Petunia, Caladium, Budleya*, ca. 1910–13
Tempera and gold leaf on canvas
10′ x 8′ 4″
The Museum of Modern Art, New York, Gift of the Eugene and Agnes E. Meyer Collection, given by their family, 1974

Joseph Stella (1877–1946)
Peonies, ca. 1911
Silverpoint and crayon on prepared paper
23⅛ x 18½″
Amon Carter Museum, Fort Worth. Gift of Ruth Carter Stevenson

Joseph Stella (1877–1946)
• *Battle of Lights, Coney Island, Mardi Gras*, 1913
Oil on canvas
75¾ x 84″
Yale University Art Gallery, Bequest of Dorothea Dreier to the Collection Société Anonyme

Joseph Stella (1877–1946)
• *Tropical Sonata*, 1919–20
Oil on canvas
48 x 29″
Whitney Museum of American Art, Purchase

Joseph Stella (1877–1946)
• *Waterlilies*, 1919–20
Oil on glass
12½ x 7″
Collection of Margaret L. Driscoll

Maurice Sterne (1878–1957)
Dancer
Black lithograph crayon on buff wove paper
16½ x 8″
Philadelphia Museum of Art, Gift of George Biddle

Maurice Sterne (1878–1957)
Bali Priestess, ca. 1913
Oil on canvas
24⅛ x 20⅜″
Philadelphia Museum of Art, The Louis E. Stern Collection

Florine Stettheimer (1871–1944)
Picnic at Bedford Hills, 1919
Oil on canvas
40 5/16 x 50¼″
Museum of American Art of the Pennsylvania Academy of the Fine Arts. Gift of Ettie Stettheimer, 1950.2

Florine Stettheimer (1871–1944)
• *Asbury Park South*, 1920
Oil on canvas
50½ x 60½″
Collection Fisk University, Nashville, Tennessee, Gift of Carl Van Vechten

Joaquín Torres-Garcia (1874–1949)
• *Fourteenth Street*, 1920
Oil on board
22 x 18″
Courtesy of CDS Gallery, New York

Abraham Walkowitz (1880–1965)
Side Show at Coney Island
Oil on canvas
26 x 40″
Collection of The Newark Museum, Gift of Abraham Walkowitz in memory of Beatrice Winser, 1953

Abraham Walkowitz (1880–1965)
New York, 1917
Watercolor, ink, and pencil on paper
30⅝ x 21¾″
Whitney Museum of American Art, Gift of the artist in memory of Juliana Force

Max Weber (1881–1961)
Abraham Walkowitz, 1907
Oil on canvas
25¼ x 20 3/16″
The Brooklyn Museum, Gift of Abraham Walkowitz 44.65

Max Weber (1881–1961)
Connecticut Landscape, 1911
Oil on canvas mounted on board
28 x 22¼″
Collection of Maurice and Margery Katz

Max Weber (1881–1961)
Yellow Urn, 1914
Charcoal and pastel on laid paper
24½ x 18½″
Collection of Mr. and Mrs. Meyer P. Potamkin

Max Weber (1881–1961)
Rush Hour, New York, 1915
Oil on canvas
36¼ x 30¼″
National Gallery of Art, Washington, D. C., Gift of the Avalon Foundation 1970.6.1

William H. K. Yarrow (1891–1941)
• *Flowers*, ca. 1920
Oil on canvas
30 x 24″
Collection of Ellen Speiser Katz

William H. K. Yarrow (1891–1941)
Mountain Landscape, ca. 1920
Watercolor on paper
9¾ x 13¾″
Courtesy of SBC Communications Inc., San Antonio, Texas

Marguerite Zorach (1887–1968)
The Connoisseur, 1910–11
Oil on canvas
22 x 17½″
Collection of Mr. and Mrs. Meyer P. Potamkin

Marguerite Zorach (1887–1968)
The Storm, ca. 1913
Watercolor over pencil on paper
12¼ x 15¾″
Collection of Mr. and Mrs. Meyer P. Potamkin

Marguerite Zorach (1887–1968)
• *Camp in the Woods*, 1920
Oil on canvas
20 x 16″
Collection of Mr. and Mrs. Irwin L. Bernstein

William Zorach (1889–1966)
• *Mirage—Ships at Night*, 1919
Oil on canvas
32½ x 26″
National Museum of American Art, Smithsonian Institution, Gift from the collection of the Zorach children

William Zorach (1889–1966)
In the Sierras, 1920
Watercolor on paper
13 x 10″
Courtesy of Zabriskie Gallery, New York

CHECKLIST
FACSIMILE

Exhibition of Paintings and Drawings Showing the Later Tendencies in Art printed checklist. Archives of the Pennsylvania Academy of the Fine Arts.

Exhibition of Paintings and Drawings Showing the Later Tendencies in Art

April 16 to May 15

The Pennsylvania Academy of the Fine Arts

PHILADELPHIA

1921

Paintings and Drawings by American Artists showing the Later Tendencies in Art

An Exhibition held by courtesy of the Pennsylvania Academy of the Fine Arts, Broad and Cherry Streets, Philadelphia.

COMMITTEE OF SELECTION

Thomas Benton
Bernard Gussow
Paul Burlin
Joseph Stella
Arthur B. Carles
Alfred Stieglitz
William Yarrow

HANGING COMMITTEE

Paul Burlin
Arthur B. Carles
Thomas Benton
Alfred Stieglitz
William Yarrow

CATALOGUE OF THE EXHIBITION

GALLERY I.

FLORINE STETTHEIMER.
1 A Day in West Point.

C. BERTRAM HARTMAN.
2 The Crown.

E. B. GROSSMAN.
3 Helen by the Sea.

J. TORRES-GARCIA.
4 Spanish Town.

JOSEPH M. GARVEY.
5 The Dance.

D. W. McCOUCH.
6 Landscape, with Church.

B. J. O. NORDFELDT.
7 Corn Dance: San Ildefonso.

ALLEN TUCKER.
8 Scherzo: A Song.

EDWARD FISK.
9 Adirondack Lake.

PRESTON DICKINSON.
10 House Forms and Landscape.

JOHN PANDICK.
11 Portrait.

SAMUEL HALPERT.
12 Interior.

JAMES H. DAUGHERTY.
13 Still Life.

JOHN PANDICK.
14 Composition.

EDWARD FISK.
15 Still Life.

GEORGE BIDDLE.
16 Allegro.

EMILE BRANCHARD.
17 The Lake.

HUGO ROBUS.
18 Fire Escapes and Things.

EDWARD NAGLE.
19 Forty-second Street, Going West.

GEORGE BIDDLE.
20 Il Penseroso.

EMILE BRANCHARD.
21 The Grove.

JAMES H. DAUGHERTY.
22 Crossing the Plains.

GEORGE F. OF.
23 Still Life.

J. TORRES-GARCIA.
24 Business Town.

RAFAEL SALA.
25 On the Mediterranean Seaboard.

MORRIS KANTOR.
26 Sunset.

RICHARD BOIX.
27 Crash.

WALTER PACH.
28 The Waterfall.

FLORINE STETTHEIMER.
29 Asbury Park, South.

RICHARD BOIX.
30 Three.

E. E. CUMMINGS.
31 Noise: Number Five.

GEORGE BIDDLE.
32 Flute Player and Ballad Singer.

KATHERINE L. DREIER.
33 Bibi.

ELIZABETH NAGEL.
34 Pastel.

JOSEPH STELLA.
35 Water Lilies.

HAMILTON EASTER FIELD.
36 Colonial.

ARNOLD FRIEDMAN.
37 Pressure.

ELIZABETH NAGEL.
38 Painting.

NORTH CORRIDOR.

BEN BENN.
39 Still Life.

HENRY FITCH TAYLOR.
40 Abstraction.

A. S. BAYLINSON.
41 Figure.

MORRIS KANTOR.
42 Quiet Waters.

ARNOLD FRIEDMAN.
43 Flight.

J. TORRES-GARCIA.
44 Fourteenth Street.

WM. ZORACH.
45 The Waterfall.

BERNARD GUSSOW.
46 The Woods.

HUGO ROBUS.
47 Promenade.

GEORGE BIDDLE.
48 Nude.

CARL NEWMAN.
49 Painting: Number One.
50 Painting: Number Three.
51 Toys.

HUNT DIEDERICH.
52 Polo: Silhouette.

MAURICE STERNE.
53 The Circus.

YASUO KUNIYOSHI.
54 Fishermen's Huts.

HUNT DIEDERICH.
55 Polo: Silhouette.

LAYMAN SAYEN.
56 Landscape.

B. J. O. NORDFELDT.
57 Father and Son.

LYMAN SAYEN.
58 Landscape.

WOOD GAYLOR.
59 Vampires.
Lent by Mrs. M. Erdrich.

A. S. BAYLINSON.
60 Figure.

HENRY FITCH TAYLOR.
61 Ave Maria.

E. E. CUMMINGS.
62 Noise: Number One.

ELIZABETH NAGEL.
63 Drawing.

EMILE BRANCHARD.
64 High Tide.
65 To the Hills.
66 Rocky Shore.

ALLEN TUCKER.
67 Portrait in Dull Red.

GALLERY H.

W. GLACKENS.
68 Finnish Woman.

RAFAEL SALA.
69 Still Life.

W. GLACKENS.
70 Avery's Point.

ROBERT LAURENT.
71 Rocks and Boat.

A. H. MAURER.
72 Head: Number Two.

NAN WATSON.
73 Still Life.
Lent by Mrs. Willard Force.

GUS MAGER.
74 Wyoming, New Jersey: Landscape.

ROBERT LAURENT.
75 Rocks and Trees.

LEON HART.
76 Brickyards on the Hudson.

WALTER PACH.
77 Portrait.

BERNARD GUSSOW.
78 Landscape.

ARTHUR B. DAVIES.
79 Strong Toil of Grace.

GEORGE F. OF.
80 Portrait.

BERNARD GUSSOW.
81 Trees.

GUS MAGER.
82 Maine Pool.

HUGO ROBUS.
83 The Concrete Mixer.

J. TORRES-GARCIA.
84 Fashion.

WOOD GAYLOR.
85 Edna.

ARTHUR B. CARLES.
86 Monotype.

VINCENT CANADÉ.
87 Still Life.

LOUIS BOUCHÉ.
88 East and West.

HOMER BOSS.
89 The Dawn.

JUSTUS PFEIFFEN.
90 Figures.

JOHN SLOAN.
91 Girl with Flowers.

WM. ZORACH.
92 Adoration.

C. BERTRAM HARTMAN.
93 Moon Path.

VINCENT CANADÉ
94 Landscape.

WILLIAM YARROW.
95 Flowers.
Lent by Mr. Maurice S. Speiser.

CHARLES DEMUTH.
96 Business.

VINCENT CANADÉ.
97 Little Trees.

MARGUERITE ZORACH.
98 Camp in the Woods.

JENNINGS TOFEL.
99 Ascending.

GEORGE CANADÉ.
100 Landscape.

ANDREW DASBURG.
101 Landscape.

VINCENT CANADÉ.
102 Landscape.

JUSTUS PFEIFFEN.
103 The Park.

MARION H. BECKETT.
104 Wyomissing Iris.

KONRAD CRAMER.
105 Man Reading.

JOHN PANDICK.
106 Still Life.

SAMUEL HALPERT.
107 Village Near the Sea.

JOHN SLOAN.
108 Etching.
109 Etching.

MACDONALD WRIGHT.
110 Painting: Number One.
Lent by Mr. Maurice J. Speiser.

JOHN SLOAN.
111 Etching.
112 Etching.

PRESTON DICKINSON.
113 Landscape: Number Two.

ANDREW DASBURG.
114 Village Street.

ALFRED J. FRUEH.
115 Drawing.

SARA CARLES.
116 Study.

SARAH LANGLEY.
117 Improvisations: Number Two.

MARION H. BECKETT.
118 Tiger Lilies.

FLORA SCHOENFELD.
119 Mountain Home: Santa Fé.

JEAN KNOX.
120 Still Life.

BEN BENN.
121 Landscape.

GEORGE F. OF.
122 Landscape.

ARTHUR G. DOVE.
123 A Walk: Poplars.
Lent by Mr. Charles Daniel.

D. W. McCOUCH.
124 Lake Maggiore.

ARTHUR G. DOVE.
125 League of Nations: 1914.
Lent by Mr. Charles Daniel.

ANDREW DASBURG.
126 Landscape.

JENNINGS TOFEL.
127 Street with Mountain.

GALLERY G.

THOMAS H. BENTON.
128 Landscape.

GASTON LACHAISE.
129 Drawing.

ALFRED J. FRUEH.
130 Drawing.

C. BERTRAM HARTMAN.
131 Village: Stonington, Maine.

PRESTON DICKINSON.
132 House Forms and Hills.

ARTHUR B. DAVIES.
133 Tragic Mask.

EDWARD FISK.
134 Mountain Lake.

JAMES H. DAUGHERTY.
135 The Hands of Moses.

ALFRED J. FRUEH.
136 Drawing.

BEN BENN.
137 Landscape.

MARGUERITE ZORACH.
138 Camp at Night.

KONRAD CRAMER.
139 Under the Tent.

CARL KAHLER.
140 A Negro Head.

GEORGIA O'KEEFFE.
141 Red.
142 Pink.
143 Black Spot.

MORRIS KANTOR.
144 Head.

CARL KAHLER.
145 A Barn.

WM. ZORACK.
146 Yosemite Landscape.

WILLIAM YARROW.
147 Man in Action.

LEON HART.
148 Germinal.

HORACE BRODZKY.
149 Water Color.

LEON HART.
150 Fructidor.

MARGUERITE ZORACH.
151 Yosemite Trails.

ARTHUR B. DAVIES.
152 Three Masks.

C. BERTRAM HARTMAN.
153 Evening Light.

CARL KAHLER.
154 Creation.

A. WALKOWITZ.
155 Drawing.

HORACE BRODZKY.
156 Water Color.
157 Peasants.
158 New Rochelle.

JOHN COVERT.
159 Resurrection.

HENRY L. MCFEE,
160 Still Life.

JOHN MARIN.
161 Weehawken
162 Woolworth Building.
163 The Brooklyn Bridge and City.
164 Brooklyn Bridge.

JOHN COVERT.
165 Temptation of St. Anthony.

THOMAS H. BENTON.
166 Study for a Decoration.

A. H. MAURER.
167 Head: Number Four.

JULES PASCIN.
168 Street Corner in New Orleans.
169 Street in Havana.
Lent by Mr. Ferdinand Howald.
170 In a Park.
Lent by Mr. Ferdinand Howald.
171 Conversation.

A. H. MAURER.
172 Head: Number Three.

CHARLES DEMUTH.
173 In Vaudeville.
Lent by Mr. Charles Daniel.

OWEN MERTON.
174 Hillside.

JOSEPH STELLA.
175 Silverpoint: 1st.
176 Silverpoint: 2nd.

OWEN MERTON.
177 Coming Storm.
178 Marseilles.

HENRY MCCARTER.
179 House of Worship.

WOOD GAYLOR.
180 Drawing.

OWEN MERTON.
181 View of Flushing.

WOOD GAYLOR.
182 Drawing.

WILLIAM YARROW.
183 Rocks.

CHARLES DEMUTH.
184 Class 5 G.

OWEN MERTOH.
185 The Village.

JOHN MARIN.
186 Moving Showers.
187 Rocks and Sea: Maine.
Lent by Mr. Alfred Stieglitz.
188 Moonlight.
189 Mountain Shapes and Sky.
190 Low Tide: Moose Island, Maine.
Lent by Mr. Alfred Stieglitz.

JOSEPH STELLA.
191 Flowers.

EDWARD FISK.
192 The Mountain.

PAUL BURLIN.
193 Concentric Energy.
194 Drawing.

EDWARD FISK.
195 The Farm.

NORTH TRANSEPT.

GASTON LACHAISE.
196 Drawing.
197 Drawing.

MAURICE STERNE.
198 Elizabeth Duncan: Dancer.

GASTON LACHAISE.
199 Drawing.
200 Drawing.

WILLIAM YARROW.
201 Flowers.

CHARLES SHEELER.
202 Still Life: Drawing.

MAURICE STERNE.
203 Seated Figure.

A. WALKOWITZ.
204 Drawing.

ANDREW DASBURG.
205 Drawing.

PAUL BURLIN.
206 Small Orchestra.

ANDREW DASBURG.
207 Drawing.

MARIUS DE ZAYAS.
208 Darnton.
Lent by Mr. Alfred Stieglitz.

CHARLES SHEELER.
209 Bucks County Barn.

GUS MAGER.
210 Farm Idyl.

MARIUS DE ZAYAS.
211 John Marin and Alfred Stieglitz.
Lent by Mr. Alfred Stieglitz.

MAURICE STERNE.
212 Taos Indian Woman.

J. PASCIN.
213 Etching.
Lent by Mr. Wood Gaylor.
214 Cuban Lovers.
Lent by Mr. Wood Gaylor.
215 Etching.
Lent by Mr. Wood Gaylor.
216 Etching.
Lent by Mr. Wood Gaylor.

ALFRED J. FRUEH.
217 Drawing.

MAURICE STERNE.
218 Dancer in Action.

MARIUS DE ZAYAS.
219 Katharine N. Rhoades.
Lent by Mr. Alfred Stieglitz.

ALFRED J. FRUEH.
220 Drawing.

MARIUS DE ZAYAS.
221 Marion Beckett.
Lent by Mr. Alfred Stieglitz.

ROBERT LAURENT.
222 Rocks.

LOUIS BOUCHÉ.
223 English Style.

KONRAD CRAMER.
224 Girl Dressing.

RAFAEL SALA.
225 A Beach of Catalonia.

BEN BENN.
226 Study of a Woman's Head.

E. B. GROSSMAN.
227 Nude Study.
228 Nude Model.

A. WALKOWITZ.
229 New York.

GALLERY F.

MORTON L. SCHAMBERG.
230 Painting: Number One.

JOHN COVERT.
231 Brass Band.

WALTER PACH.
232 Sunday Night.

MARSDEN HARTLEY.
233 Still Life: Black Leaves.

WALT KUHN.
234 The City.

S. MACDONALD WRIGHT.
235 Aeroplane: Synchromy in Yellow and Orange.

EMILE BRANCHARD.
236 Old Chestnuts.

LOUIS BOUCHÉ.
237 Portrait: Horace Brodzky.

MAX WEBER.
238 Portrait.

EMILE BRANCHARD.
239 Birch Trees.

PRESTON DICKINSON.
240 Landscape: Number One.

A. S. BAYLINSON.
241 Figure.

ARTHUR B. DAVIES.
242 On Violence.
243 Mænad Arabesque.

JOSEPH STELLA.
244 Battle of Light: Coney Island.

MAN RAY.
245 MCMXIV.

MAURICE STERNE.
246 Flower in Vase.

BERNARD GUSSOW.
247 Passing Figures.

LOUIS BOUCHÉ.
248 Still Life.

HOMER BOSS.
249 The Red Fog.

JOHN MARIN.
250 Tree Form.

S. MACDONALD WRIGHT.
251 Synchromy.
Lent by Mr. Jacob Dewald.

EDWARD J. STEICHEN.
252 Mural Decoration: Fragment.
Lent by Mr. Eugene Meyer, Jr.

MARSDEN HARTLEY.
253 Flowers in Glass.

MAX WEBER.
254 Chinese Restaurant.

MARSDEN HARTLEY.
255 Landscape: New Mexico.

THOMAS H. BENTON.
256 The Beach.

MARSDEN HARTLEY.
257 Movement: Provincetown.

EDWARD J. STEICHEN.
258 Mural Decoration: Fragment.
Lent by Mr. Eugene Meyer, Jr.

CHARLES SHEELER.
259 Bucks County Barn.

JOSEPH M. GARVEY.
260 The Masked Ball.

WM. ZORACH.
261 Ships Passing at Night.

CHARLES SHEELER.
262 New York.

LOUIS BOUCHÉ.
263 Still Life.

WM. ZORACH.
264 Interior and Exterior.

WILLIAM YARROW.
265 Shadow-Boxer.

D. W. MCCOUCH.
266 Village Entrance.

ARTHUR B. DAVIES.
267 Façade.

GEORGE F. OF.
268 The Church.

MAN RAY.
269 Departure of Summer.

CHARLES DEMUTH.
270 Aucassin and Nicolette.
Lent by Mrs. Meredith Hare.

PAUL BURLIN.
271 Awakening.
Lent by Mr. George A. Harris.

CHARLES DEMUTH.
272 From the Garden of the Château.

HENRY L. MCFEE.
273 Portrait of a Painter.

CARL KAHLER.
274 A Mechanism.

ARTHUR B. CARLES.
275 Profile.

MORTON L. SCHAMBERG.
276 Painting: Number Two.

WALT KUHN.
277 Youth.
Lent by Mr. John Quinn.

JOSEPH STELLA.
278 Tropical Sonata.

WOOD GAYLOR.
279 Posters.

MORTON L. SCHAMBERG.
280 Painting: Number Three.

INDEX TO ARTISTS

REPRESENTED IN THE PRESENT EXHIBITION.

The figures following the address refer to the numbers in this catalogue.

30

INDEX.

31

INDEX.

32

INDEX.

33

Photograph Credits

Scott Bowron: p. 10, fig. 2

Rick Echelmeyer: p. 11, fig. 4; p. 12, fig. 5; p. 13, fig. 6; p. 14, figs. 8–9; p. 15, fig. 10; p. 17, fig. 12; p. 20, figs. 17–19; p. 21, fig. 20; p. 27, fig. 1; p. 29, fig. 3; p. 31, fig. 7; p. 32, fig. 8; p. 37; p. 43; pp. 48–49; p. 56; pp. 62–63.